OSPREY
PUBLISHING

The Lines of Torres Vedras 1809–11

Ian Fletcher · Illustrated by Bill Younghusband

Series editors Marcus Cowper and Nikolai Bogdanovic

First published in Great Britain in 2003 by Osprey Publishing, Elms Court, Chapel Way, Botley, Oxford OX2 9LP, United Kingdom.
Email: info@ospreypublishing.com

ISBN 1 84176 576 7

Editorial by Ilios Publishing, Oxford, UK (www.iliospublishing.com)
Maps by Map Studio, Romsey, UK
Index by Alison Worthington
Proofreading: Bob Munro
Design: Ken Vail Graphic Design, Cambridge, UK
Originated by Grasmere Digital Imaging, Leeds, UK
Printed and bound by L-Rex Printing Company Ltd

03 04 05 06 07   10 9 8 7 6 5 4 3 2 1

A CIP catalogue record for this book is available from the British Library.

FOR A CATALOGUE OF ALL BOOKS PUBLISHED BY OSPREY MILITARY
AND AVIATION PLEASE CONTACT:

Osprey Direct UK, P.O. Box 140, Wellingborough,
Northants, NN8 2FA, UK
E-mail: info@ospreydirect.co.uk

Osprey Direct USA, c/o MBI Publishing, P.O. Box 1,
729 Prospect Ave, Osceola, WI 54020, USA
E-mail: info@ospreydirectusa.com

www.ospreypublishing.com

Artist's note

Readers may care to note that the original paintings from which the colour plates in this book were prepared are available for private sale. All reproduction copyright whatsoever is retained by the Publishers. All enquiries should be addressed to:

Bill Younghusband
Moorfield,
Kilcolman West
Buttevant, Co. Cork
Eire

The Publishers regret that they can enter into no correspondence upon this matter.

Acknowledgement

The author would like to express his thanks to John Strecker, who took many of the modern photos that appear in this work of the Lines of Torres Vedras.

Contents

Introduction

Sir Richard Fletcher, Bart. (1768–1813). Wellington's chief engineer and the man behind the construction of the Lines of Torres Vedras. Fletcher was killed at the storming of San Sebastian in 1813.

When Napoleon Bonaparte sent General Andoche Junot over the Pyrenees into Spain at the head of 25,000 French troops in October 1807, he did so not knowing that he was committing his armed forces to a conflict which they would never really master; a conflict that would, over the next six and a half years, become a constant drain on the resources of his empire. Spain was not Junot's intended objective; that dubious distinction fell to Portugal, where Junot hoped to impose his emperor's Continental System on the Portuguese king and his government. Portugal, one of Britain's allies, had steadfastly refused to implement the blockade of British trade and so was about to pay for its sin against the French empire.

Junot arrived in Lisbon in November 1807, but failed to arrest the Portuguese royal family, which sailed off to the safety of Brazil. In the meantime, Portugal was placed in the hands of Napoleon's lieutenants, as was Spain the following year. Tired of the bickering between King Carlos IV and his son, Ferdinand, Napoleon summoned them to Bayonne where he had both men arrested. Madrid was occupied by Joachim Murat and in May 1808 risings in the capital were ruthlessly suppressed, causing a backlash against the French throughout the country. The Iberian nations appealed to Britain for help, and so it was that in August 1808, Sir Arthur Wellesley, the future Duke of Wellington, landed in Portugal at the head of 9,000 British troops. These were the first steps along an extremely long and at times painful road that would eventually lead them to Toulouse, in southern France, which they entered in triumph after a campaign that was to last six years.

The war in the Iberian Peninsula had been raging for just over two years before the subject of this book, the Lines of Torres Vedras, began to make a dramatic and crucial impact on events. Following their landings in Portugal, the British Army had enjoyed mixed fortunes. The initial battles of the war were fought shortly after the 9,000-strong army had been joined by a further 5,000 troops who had sailed up from Gibraltar under the command of Sir Brent

Spencer. On 17 August 1808, Wellesley's force brushed aside a numerically inferior French force, commanded by General Delaborde, at the small village of Rolica. The battle, a skirmish by later standards, was followed four days later by a much more important and impressive victory at Vimeiro, where for the first time on a Peninsular battlefield, lines of British infantry demonstrated the advantages gained by fighting in such a formation against French columns. The defeat of a French Napoleonic army was a rare event indeed; and if in England church bells sounded in victory around the country, the only bells that rang in France were ones of alarm. The war in the Peninsula was never regarded by Napoleon as being anything more than a sideshow, but the British victory at Vimeiro did not go unnoticed by many of his generals who would feel the power of British musketry on many a dusty battlefield during the next six years.

The short-term result of Wellesley's victory at Vimeiro was the infamous Convention of Cintra. Trapped against the Lisbon Peninsula, with the Tagus in their rear and to the right, and with the Atlantic to their left, the French sued for an armistice, which they concluded to their advantage. Sir Hew Dalrymple and Sir Harry Burrard, two British generals who had arrived in Portugal to take over from Wellesley, along with an apparently unwilling and reluctant Wellesley, negotiated the final treaty known as the Convention of Cintra, which allowed the French to escape from what they themselves called 'a mousetrap'. The treaty allowed the French to sail back to France with their accumulated arms and plunder, but worse, they were taken back to France in the ships of the Royal Navy. Naturally, this was all too much for the British government, who were appalled by the fact that, instead of destroying the French army, the British generals had given them a ride home. The fact that the French had given up all the fortresses in Portugal without the British army having to conduct lengthy siege operations appears to have escaped them. The fact remains that, in early 19th-century Britain, enemy armies were there to be destroyed, not helped home. With this in mind, Dalrymple and Burrard were recalled to face a court of inquiry, Wellesley already having gone home on leave anyway.

In the meantime, the British Army in Portugal was placed under the command of Sir John Moore, one of Britain's finest soldiers. Moore had been instrumental in the development of light infantry in addition to which he had introduced lasting reforms regarding the internal discipline of infantry battalions. Nevertheless, when he led his army into Spain in order to help the Spanish insurgents, he found himself quickly overtaken by events in the country as Napoleon himself came south across the Pyrenees to chase Moore and his army into the sea. In the event, he failed and turned back, leaving the

Maj.Gen. Robert Craufurd, (1764–1812). 'Black Bob', as he was known, commanded the Light Division from 1810 until his death at Ciudad Rodrigo in January 1812. His division was the most active of Wellington's divisions throughout the spring and summer of 1810 during the period of the Lines' construction.

pursuit of Moore to Marshal Soult, who led his men through the snows of the Galician mountains, driving Moore's retreating army all the way to Corunna. Here, on 16 January 1809, Moore and his bedraggled army turned to fight their tormentors: Moore's victory allowed them to re-embark in the ships of the Royal Navy in an operation not dissimilar to Dunkirk over 130 years later. Sadly, Moore was not with them when they sailed back to England. He had been mortally wounded by a French cannon ball during the battle, and whilst his army sailed home, he was left 'alone with his glory' on the ramparts of Corunna.

In April 1809, having been acquitted of all charges relating to the Convention of Cintra, Sir Arthur Wellesley returned to Portugal to assume command of the British Army there. Within four weeks he had driven the French from Portugal for a second time. He defeated Soult at Oporto, and then struck south to confront a much larger French army: at Talavera on 27–28 July he fought what was to be the bloodiest battle of the war, save for Albuera. The battle, fought over a day and a night, ended in a costly victory for Wellesley, and not only demonstrated once again the power of British linear tactics over the French column, but showed that co-operation with his Spanish allies was fraught with difficulties. The victory yielded few positive results for Wellesley, although it did gain him the title 'Wellington', and he was forced to retreat to the safety of the Portuguese border in the area between the twin fortresses of Ciudad Rodrigo and Almeida.

Marshal Andre Masséna, Prince of Essling (1758–1817). Known as 'The Fox', Wellington regarded Masséna as his most dangerous enemy in the Peninsula. He was the biggest loser during the campaign of 1810–11. Worn out by years of constant campaigning, Masséna, a pale shadow of the man who had distinguished himself on many a campaign, proved totally unable to find a way of breaking through the Lines and was eventually forced into a harrowing retreat in the early spring of 1811.

It would be 14 months before Wellington's army fought its next major battle, during which time the army sat and waited on the border, whilst at home the voices of those opposed to the war in Spain grew ever louder. Doubts were even raised in Wellington's own camp. Many of his own officers, who were known to him as 'croakers', questioned both the wisdom of doing nothing and the cause in Spain itself. After all, the Spaniards appeared to be doing little to help themselves, and all they ever read in the papers and in despatches was news of more disasters befalling the Spanish armies.

However, unknown to virtually all of his army, both officers and men alike, was the fact that while the army was preparing to meet the expected French invasion of Portugal, thousands of Portuguese workmen were working frantically to complete what has been described as both one of the cheapest investments and best-kept secrets in military history – the Lines of Torres Vedras.

ABOVE **The 1st Foot Guards at Ramsgate, preparing to sail for the** Peninsula in September 1808. The regiment arrived too late to take part in the battles of Rolica and Vimeiro, but unfortunately was in time for the retreat to Corunna.

BELOW The battlefield of Rolica, Wellington's (still Wellesley at the time) first victory in the Peninsula. This is the view from Delaborde's initial position, looking north from Rolica itself towards Óbidos.

ABOVE The 3rd Foot Guards in action during the Battle of Talavera, 27–28 July 1809. Fourteen months were to pass before Wellington fought his next battle (at Busaco) during the retreat to the Lines.

BELOW The Battle of Busaco, 27 September 1810. This was the one great battle during Wellington's retreat to the Lines, and although he was victorious he never entertained the notion of following it up and driving the French back towards Spain. French apologists claim a victory for Masséna, on account of the fact that he found a way round Wellington's left flank after the battle, causing the Allies to withdraw in greater haste than they would otherwise have done.

Chronology

1807

18 October	French troops under General Andoche Junot cross the Spanish border, marching south to Lisbon.
30 November	French troops occupy the Portuguese capital, Lisbon.

1808

23 March	French troops occupy the Spanish capital, Madrid.
2 May	The *Dos de Mayo* insurrection in Madrid. Other risings follow throughout May and June.
1 August	Sir Arthur Wellesley and his troops land at the mouth of the River Mondego in Portugal.
17 August	Wellesley defeats Delaborde at Rolica.
21 August	Wellesley is victorious again, this time at Vimeiro: he is superseded by Dalrymple and Burrard. The Convention of Cintra follows, and the French are able to negotiate a favourable armistice. They sail home in the ships of the Royal Navy. Burrard and Dalrymple are recalled, but Wellesley has already returned home.
18–26 October	The British Army, now under the command of Sir John Moore, begins its advance form Lisbon.
10 December	Moore advances from Salamanca.
21 December	Paget is victorious at Sahagun. He follows this up with another victory, at Benavente on 29 December.

1809

16 January	The Battle of Corunna. The British Army defeats Soult at Corunna, but Moore is mortally wounded. The victory allows the British to sail back to England.
22 April	Wellesley is once again in command in Portugal.
12 May	Wellesley captures Oporto. Soult is thrown out of Portugal.
27–28 July	Wellesley achieves a costly victory at Talavera. He is rewarded with a peerage, and the name 'Wellington'.
20 October	Wellington issues his Memorandum for the construction of the Lines of Torres Vedras.

1810

10 July	Ciudad Rodrigo falls to the French under Marshal Masséna.
24 July	The Combat of the Côa: Robert Craufurd and his Light Division are severely tested on the Côa as the French invasion gathers momentum.
26 August	Almeida is devastated by a huge explosion as the magazine blows up. The town surrenders to the French shortly afterwards.
27 September	Wellington defeats Ney and Masséna at Busaco. A rearguard action, it delays Masséna for only a short time before the French find their way round the Allied right flank.
9 October	Wellington's troops begin to take up positions in the Lines of Torres Vedras.
14 November	Masséna withdraws to Santarém in order to procure fresh supplies.

1811

5 March	Masséna begins his retreat north towards the Mondego.
11 March	Combat at Pombal, the first in a series of fights between Wellington and the retreating French.
12 March	Combat at Redinha.
14 March	Combat at Cazal Nova.
15 March	Combat at Foz d'Arouce.
3 April	Combat at Sabugal, the last action of Masséna's retreat.
3–5 May	Battle of Fuentes de Oñoro, Masséna's last battle in Spain and the effective end of the third French invasion of Portugal.

The Lines of Torres Vedras, October 1810

This illustration shows the layout of the Lines, the main military districts, and the main allied deployments in October 1810. The inset detail at top right shows the situation in the Iberian Peninsula in 1810, and the territory held by the respective powers. The military districts of the Lines are listed below, together with their troop complements.

No. 1: from Torres Vedras to the sea.
HQ: Torres Vedras
2,470 Militia Infantry
250 Ordenanza Artillery
140 Portuguese Line Artillery
70 British Artillery

No.2: from Sobral to the valley of the Calhandrix
HQ: Sobral
1,300 Militia Infantry
300 Ordenanza Artillery
140 Portuguese Line Artillery
40 British Artillery

No.3: from Alhandra to the valley of the Calhandrix
HQ: Alhandra
400 Militia Infantry
60 Ordenanza Artillery
60 British Artillery

No.4: from the banks of the River Tagus near Alverca to the pass of Bucellas
HQ: Bucellas
1,100 Militia Infantry
500 Ordenanza Artillery
80 Portuguese Line Artillery

No.5: from the pass of Freixal to the pass of Mafra
HQ: Montachique
2,400 Militia Infantry
480 Ordenanza Artillery
120 Portuguese Line Artillery
50 British Artillery

No.6: from Mafra to the sea
HQ: Mafra
700 Militia Infantry
350 Ordenanza Artillery
230 Portuguese Line Artillery
40 British Artillery

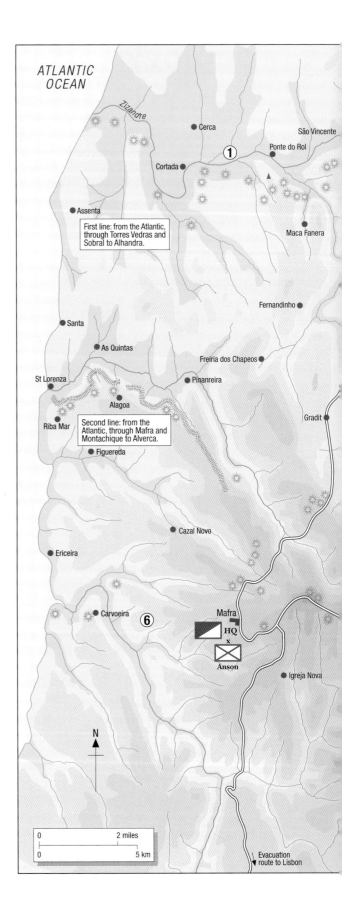

First line: from the Atlantic, through Torres Vedras and Sobral to Alhandra.

Second line: from the Atlantic, through Mafra and Montachique to Alverca.

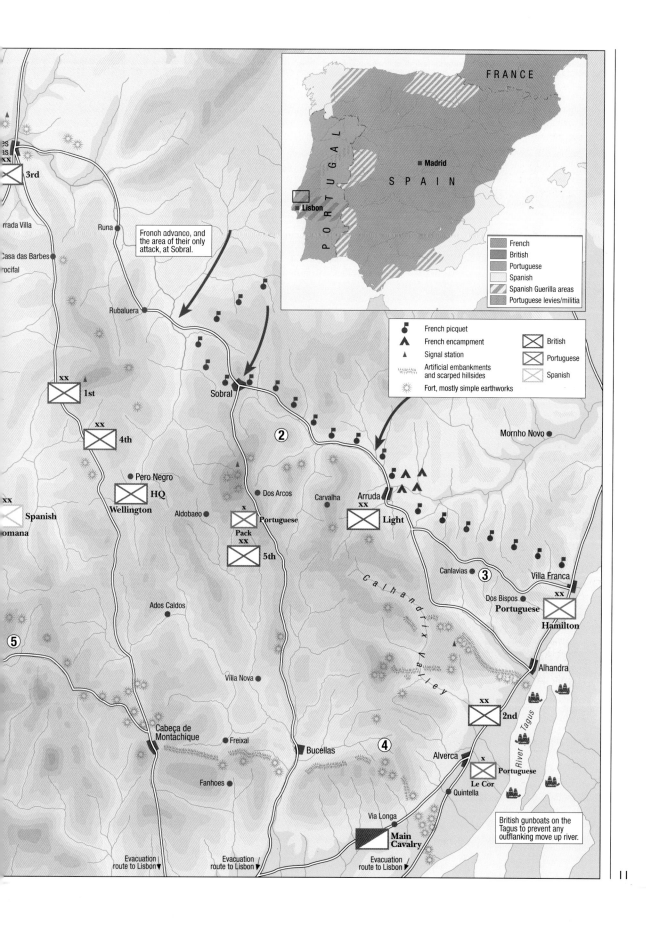

3rd

rrada Villa

Runa

Casa das Barbes
rocifal

Fronch advance, and the area of their only attack, at Sobral.

Rubaluera

1st

4th

Pero Negro

HQ
Wellington

Aldobaeo

x
Portuguese
Pack
5th

Dos Arcos

Carvalha

Spanish
omana

Ados Caldos

Villa Nova

Cabeça de Montachique

Freixal

Fanhoes

Via Longa

Main Cavalry

Sobral

②

Arruda

Light

Canlavias ③

Dos Bispos

Portuguese

Hamilton

Mornho Novo

Villa Franca

Alhandra

2nd

Alverca

x
Portuguese

Le Cor

Quintella

④

Bucellas

⑤

FRANCE

Madrid

SPAIN

P O R T U G A L

■ Lisbon

French
British
Portuguese
Spanish
Spanish Guerilla areas
Portuguese levies/militia

French picquet
French encampment
Signal station
Artificial embankments and scarped hillsides
Fort, mostly simple earthworks

British
Portuguese
Spanish

Calhandrix valley

River Tagus

British gunboats on the Tagus to prevent any outflanking move up river.

Design and development

The idea of using the surrounding hills as a means to defend the Portuguese capital, Lisbon, was not a new one. Wellington may well be credited with the most successful use of this natural barrier but its strength was obvious to anyone possessing a sound military mind. A Portuguese major, Jose Maria das Neves Costa, is often cited as being the originator of the conception of the Lines, having conducted an extensive survey of the hills north of Lisbon towards the end of 1808. However, the singular characteristics of the hills had been noted late in the previous century. Costa's own plans to utilise the hills as a means of defence against future French invasions were submitted to the Portuguese government the following spring, information that was subsequently passed on to Wellington himself. But although it is usually stated that Wellington began his plans for the defence of Lisbon in October 1809 he had, in fact, already began to mull over such plans as early as September 1808.

During the lull in hostilities caused by the Cintra negotiations, Wellington took the opportunity of riding round the hills around Torres Vedras, and, with his usual expert eye for ground, made extensive observations on how the hills to the north of Lisbon leant themselves superbly to the defence of the capital. Thus,

Maj.Gen. William Carr Beresford (1764–1854). Wellington's preferred choice of second-in-command in the Peninsula. Beresford played a prominent part in the reorganisation and training of the Portuguese army in the Peninsula.

ABOVE A typical Napoleonic field work, a star-shaped fortification on the Mouiz plateau on top of the Rhune mountain as part of the French defences along the Nivelle. The fort is a superb example of the art of field fortification, although its stone construction is not typical of such forts: the majority were earthworks, as were most of the forts along the Lines of Torres Vedras.

BELOW Another typical earthwork, the Santa Barbe redoubt, again on the French line of the Nivelle. This redoubt is very similar to the forts constructed by the Allies along the Lines of Torres Vedras. Note the angles of the ditch.

This fine Napoleonic earthwork was built by the Spaniards to guard the pass at Roncesvalles. It is another example of the sort of field work thrown up by armies in the Peninsula. It takes the form of a star, has strong ramparts and a very deep ditch.

when the report submitted by Neves Costa came to him he was already fully aware of the advantages to be gained from fortifying the hills. In fact, throughout the spring of 1809, even whilst he was in the throes of driving the French from Portugal, he had begun making plans for the defence of the upper River Tagus, whilst making recommendations to the British government that guns be sent to Portugal for the specific purpose of the defence of the Lisbon Peninsula.

The real planning began in October 1809 though. With his army in position behind the Portuguese border and with the Light Division acting as a sentinel between the Agueda and Côa rivers, Wellington took himself off to Lisbon where, in the company of his chief engineer, Colonel Richard Fletcher, and the Quartermaster Generals of his own army and that of the Portuguese army, he carried out a thorough survey of the 30-mile-wide position between the Atlantic at the mouth of the River Zizandre and Alhandra on the Tagus. Throughout the first week of October he issued orders for the movement of troops to the redoubts that had already been constructed even before the issue of his now-famous memorandum of 20 October. Indeed, it is clear from Wellington's despatches that extensive work had already begun on several of the forts.

On 22 October 1809, one of Fletcher's engineers, Lieutenant Rice Jones, wrote to his father, informing him of the work going on to the north of Lisbon. The tone and content of the letter clearly indicate the secrecy that surrounded the construction of the Lines, for although Jones was aware of Wellington's intentions regarding the defence of Lisbon, he appears to have had little idea of the eventual extent of the Lines. He wrote:

Lord Viscount Wellington set out from Badajoz for this place [Lisbon] on the 8th instant, accompanied by a few of his staff, the Qr.-Mr.-Genl. And our Chief [Fletcher] in whose suite I have travelled thus far, together with

The construction of one of the forts in the Lines

Two British Royal Engineers officers are shown supervising Portuguese workmen: they will not remain long at the fort, and will depart once construction is under way, returning from time to time to check progress. In the lower level, the men are digging out the ditch at the base of the counterscarp, while on the upper level the men are hammering down the earth to form the banks of the ramparts. An armed Portuguese volunteer from the Algarve Volunteers also oversees proceedings.

More views of typical Napoleonic fieldworks at the French fort on the Mouiz plateau on the Rhune mountain. The top picture shows the interior of the fort, complete with firestep. The below picture is a view of the fort from the French defences on the Lesser Rhune.

Capt. Chapman. There are a number of reports on the subject of this visit. I know that his Lordship and the Col. have been riding all over the country for 30 miles round, and have nearly knocked up Col. Fletcher's stud; from which it is easy to conclude that the ground to be occupied for the defence of Lisbon is a material part of the Commander of the Forces' business at this place. I will also tell you what is an impenetrable secret at present even to our officers; viz., that all our Corps are ordered from the army to a place called Castanheira, about 30 miles higher up and on the same side of the Tagus as this city. The Col. talks of setting out for Castanheira tomorrow or the next day; I of course shall accompany him, and understand are a great number of works in contemplation.

So what of the hills themselves? They were, in the words of Fortescue, the historian of the British Army, 'nothing so much as a gigantic mountain-torrent instantaneously converted into solid earth.' The hills formed two main lines, with a third covering an area close to the Tagus to the west of Lisbon where any re-embarkation might have to take place. The first line stretched from Alhandra on the Tagus, west to Sobral, to Torres Vedras and the mouth of the River Zizandre, whilst the more southerly extended again from Alhandra to Mafra and on to Ribamar on the Atlantic. There was a fourth line of defences on the southern bank of the Tagus, although this chain was comparatively short and was intended simply to prevent the French threatening Lisbon from the south. There were effectively only four roads through the hills, being through Mafra via Torres Vedras, Montachique via Torres Vedras, Bucellas via Sobral, and the road along the bank of the Tagus at Alhandra. Like the Pyrenees, there were stretches where any light infantrymen could pass with ease, although, again like the Pyrenees, it was equally impossible for wheeled vehicles, artillery and cavalry to pass. The major difference between the hills to the north of Lisbon and those in northern Spain was that, unlike the latter, most of the hills in Portugal (once fortified by Wellington) bristled with guns, forts and heavily armed infantry. They would prove to be totally impassable whereas the Pyrenees were breached by the French and, indeed, by Wellington's army itself, with relative ease in 1813.

As a result of his previous reconnaissance, and in particular that undertaken with Fletcher in early October 1809, Wellington was satisfied with his arrangements for the defence of Lisbon, using the hills as the pillars of defence. And so, on 20 October, he issued to Fletcher his Memorandum for the construction of what were to become known as the Lines of Torres Vedras. In addition to the actual points regarding the forts themselves, Wellington made quite clear the object of the massive exercise. 'The great object in Portugal,' he wrote, 'is the possession of Lisbon and the Tagus, and all our measures must be directed to that object. There is another also connected with that first object, to which we must likewise attend, viz., the embarkation of the British troops in case of a reverse.'

This give us a clear insight into two of Wellington's major priorities. Almost certainly mindful of what happened to Moore earlier the same year, Wellington was determined that, in the event of a retreat he would have a safe haven to head for. Britain had only one field army, and he was its commander. He simply couldn't afford to lose it or see it disintegrate in the way that Moore's army had. When historians criticise Wellington for being defensive and cautious he was, in fact, simply being a realist. It was no good leading his army carelessly into war only to lose it and put Britain into a position from which she might never recover. Moore himself had considered Portugal indefensible, with the longest open frontier in Europe. He was probably correct, and the point was not lost on Wellington. However it was never Wellington's intention to fight for Portugal on its border, rather to defend it in the strong position in the hills to the north of Lisbon. With the Lines in his favour, he could make it impossible for an invading army to linger for any great length of time.

It went without saying that the maintenance of the Tagus was of paramount importance. As long as Britannia ruled the waves Wellington's army would be supplied through Lisbon – unlike the French invaders, whose policy of living off the land would soon be proved to be fatally flawed. Lisbon and the Tagus were, therefore, of vital importance. In fact, the role of the Royal Navy would prove to be an absolutely crucial one. The navy would bring in ship loads of supplies, not only for Wellington and his army, but for the population of Lisbon itself, and the thousands of refugees who would seek shelter within the Lines and in Lisbon after having given up their homes in the face of the French invasion.

The concept of the Lines of Torres Vedras as the keystone to Wellington's defence of Portugal is thus simple to understand. But what of their actual development? We can do no better than to list the 21 main points in Wellington's Memorandum to Fletcher that refer specifically to the construction of the forts and redoubts which formed the core of the system. It should not be forgotten that several works had already been constructed before Fletcher was issued with his instructions. But, as Wellington stated, 'in order to strengthen the several positions, it is necessary that different works should be constructed immediately, and that arrangements and preparations should be made for the construction of others. Accordingly, I beg Colonel Fletcher as soon as possible to review the several positions.' They were as follows:

He [Fletcher] will examine particularly the effect of damming up the mouth of the Castanheira river, how far it will render the river a barrier, and what extent it will fill.

He will calculate the labour required for that work, and the time it will take, as well as the means of destroying the bridge over the river, and of constructing such redoubts as might be necessary on the plain, and on the hill on the left of the road, effectually to defend the plain. He will state particularly what means should be prepared for these works. He will also consider of the means and time required, and the effect which might be produced by scarping the banks of the river.

He will make the same calculations for the works to be executed on the hill in front, and on the right of Cadafoes; particularly on the left of that hill, to shut the entry of the valley of Cadafoes.

He will examine and report upon the means of making a good road of communication from the plain across the hills with the valley of the Cadafoes and the left of the proposed position, and calculate the time and labour it will take.

He will examine the road from Otta Abringola, Labourgeira to Merciana, and thence to Torres Vedras; and also from Merciana to Sobral de Monte Agraca. He will also examine and report upon the road from Alemquer to Sobral de Monte Agraca.

He will entrench a post at Torres Vedras for 5000 men. He will examine the road from Torres Vedras to Cabeca de Montachique, and fix upon the spots at which to break it up might stop or delay the enemy; and if there should be advantageous ground at such spots, &., will entrench a position for 4000 men, to cover the retreat of the corps from Torres Vedras.

He will examine the position of Cabeca de Montachique, and determine upon its line of defence, and upon the works to be constructed for its defence by a corps of 5000, of which he will estimate the time and labour.

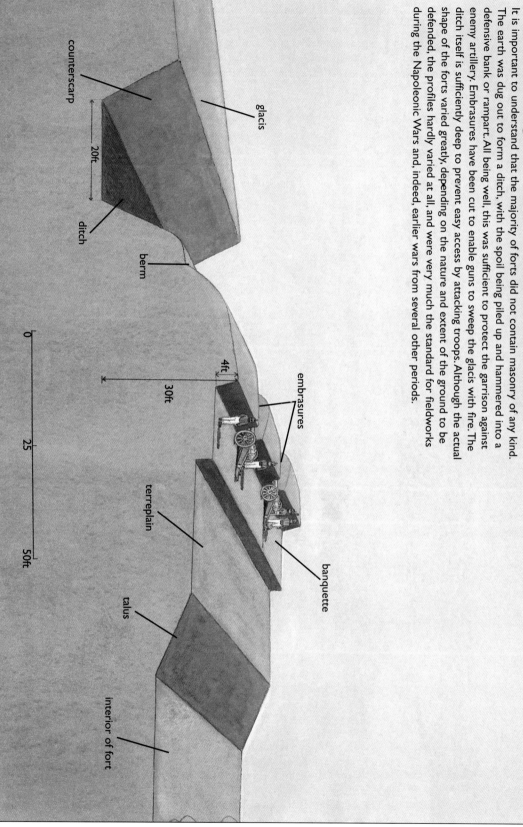

A cross-section through the earthworks of the Great Redoubt at Sobral

It is important to understand that the majority of forts did not contain masonry of any kind. The earth was dug out to form a ditch, with the spoil being piled up and hammered into a defensive bank or rampart. All being well, this was sufficient to protect the garrison against enemy artillery. Embrasures have been cut to enable guns to sweep the glacis with fire. The ditch itself is sufficiently deep to prevent easy access by attacking troops. Although the actual shape of the forts varied greatly, depending on the nature and extent of the ground to be defended, the profiles hardly varied at all, and were very much the standard for fieldworks during the Napoleonic Wars and, indeed, earlier wars from several other periods.

glacis

counterscarp

20ft

ditch

berm

4ft

30ft

embrasures

terreplain

banquette

0

25

50ft

talus

interior of fort

WRy. 03

He will entrench a position for 4000 on the two heights which command the road from Sobral de Monte Agraca [Graca] to Bucellas. He will entrench a position for 400 men on the height of St Ajuda, between Sobral and Bucellas, to cover the retreat of the corps from Sobral to Bucellas; and he will calculate the means and the time it will take to destroy the road at that spot.

He will construct a redoubt for 200 men and three guns at the windmill on the height bearing east-by-south and east-south-east from the height of Sobral de Monte Agraca; which guns will bear upon the road from Sobral to Arruda.

He will ascertain the points at which and the means by which the road from Sobral to Arruda can be destroyed.

He will ascertain the time and labour required to entrench a position which he will fix upon for 2000 men, to defend the road coming out of Arruda towards Villa Franca and Alhandra.

He will fix upon the spots at which the road from Arruda to Alhandra can be destroyed with advantage.

He will construct a redoubt on the hill which commands the road from Arruda, about one league in front of Alhandra.

He will examine the little rivers at Alhandra, and see whether, by damming them up at the mouths, he could increase the difficulties of a passage by that place; and he will ascertain the time, labour, and means which this work will require.

He will fix upon the spots and ascertain the time and labour required to construct redoubts upon the hill of Alhandra on the right, and prevent the passage of the enemy by the high road, and on the left, and in the rear, to prevent by their fire the occupation of the mountains towards Alverca.

He will determine upon the works to be constructed on the right of the position upon the Serra de Serves, as above pointed out, to prevent the enemy from forcing that point; and he will calculate the means and the time required to execute them. He will likewise examine the pass of Bucellas, and fix upon the works to be constructed for its defence, and calculate the means, time, and labour required for their execution.

He will calculate the means, time, and labour required to construct a work on the hill on which a windmill stands, at the southern entrance of the pass of Bucellas.

He will fix upon the spots on which signal-posts can be erected upon these hills to communicate from one of these positions to the other.

It is very desirable that we should have an accurate plan of this ground.

Examine the island in the river opposite Alhandra, and fix upon the spot and calculate the means and time required to construct batteries upon it, and play upon the approach to Alhandra.

Examine the effect of damming up the river which runs by Loures, and calculate the time and means required to break the bridge at Loures.

The task set for Fletcher was a massive one. It wasn't made any easier by the fact that there were few Royal Engineer officers with the army, something which dogged Wellington's operations – particularly siege operations – throughout the Peninsular War. Nevertheless, Fletcher was the most capable engineer Wellington possessed and in the event he rose to the occasion magnificently. Assisted by a handful of British and King's German Legion engineer officers, the supervision of the construction of the Lines went remarkably well.

The actual construction of the Lines was carried out by an army of Portuguese peasants, augmented by the militia. The peasants were paid the princely sum of six vintems per day as labourers and twelve as mechanics, whilst the militia worked for just one third of these rates. As the work grew and the employment became almost full-time, the peasants' pay rose to ten vintems per day as labourers. Remarkably, the entire workforce was supervised by no more than 17 engineer officers, 11 British, two KGL and four Portuguese. The engineers were assisted by 18 of their own men, whilst 150 soldiers from various line regiments were detached to assist also. As Jones, himself an engineer officer, wrote:

> In some of the districts a subaltern officer of engineers, with that small number of English soldiers [2–3] utterly ignorant of the language, directed and controlled the labours of a thousand or fifteen hundred peasantry, compelled to work, many at the distance of forty miles from their homes, whilst their own lands lay neglected … nevertheless, during a twelvemonth of this forced labour, not a single instance of insubordination or riot occurred, and the great quantity of work performed should, in justice to the Portuguese, be more ascribed to regular habits of persevering labour in those employed, than to the efficiency of the control exercised over them.

It is sometimes thought that the Lines formed one continuous barrier, similar to Hadrian's Wall or the Great Wall of China, but this was not the case, nor was it ever Wellington's intention that it should be so. Blessed with a natural barrier, all that Wellington and Fletcher had to do was to decide how to assist nature and strengthen the natural features even further. A major priority was the destruction of all roads leading to the Lines and those that ran parallel in front of them. After all, there was no sense in allowing the enemy to approach unhindered. The destruction of all bridges was another priority. In fact, anything that could be done to retard the forward movements of the French was done. Wellington also, and very controversially, initiated a scorched earth policy, which we will discuss later.

Once the French had been denied ease of approach and access, the next task was to block all valleys and passes: this was made possible by constructing dams, by the placement of huge barriers of felled trees, and by building stone walls, something which the Light Division did at Arruda. What Wellington would have given for barbed wire we will never know, but he was constructing a defensive position the likes of which would have been appreciated by those commanding armies in World War I. After all, Wellington, like Haig a century later, was simply preparing himself for a war of attrition.

Notwithstanding the natural strength of the hills to the north of Lisbon, Wellington and Fletcher identified several places where man could assist nature. To the west of Bucellas, for example, in the second line, the hillside was scarped away by blasting. Not only did they wish to make the ascent of the Allied position steeper than it already was, but they wished to deny the French any points where they may rally their troops in the event of a failed assault, and to remove the dead ground and sheltered spots. Thus, the already steep approach to the hills was made almost vertical by the removal of hundreds of tons of earth, changing the profile of these particular hills forever.

Another of the French forts on the Lesser Rhune, which still survive today. Like the fort on the Mouiz plateau the fort bears testament to the tremendous effort the French made, hauling hundreds of stones to the summit during construction. The Portuguese workmen put no less effort into the construction of the Lines of Torres Vedras.

But despite these natural and artificial barriers, both Wellington and Fletcher knew that men and artillery, firmly positioned inside strong forts and redoubts, would almost certainly be the deciding factor if the French ever did attack. Thus the work that had already begun prior to October 1809 was stepped up as the initial series of redoubts blossomed into a massive and extremely extensive range of fortifications, all of which were designed to be mutually supporting in the event of an enemy attack.

A massive undertaking, the construction of the Lines took just over one year, from the date of Wellington's Memorandum until the date of their occupation by Wellington's army. The construction has often been referred to as one of the best-kept secrets in military history. The Lines certainly came as a massive shock to Masséna when he arrived in front of them in October 1810. '*Que diable*', he is reputed to have said on seeing them for the first time. Jean Jacques Pelet, one of Masséna's aides, heard reports of the Lines during the French advance but, like most of his comrades, was sceptical of both their extent and their effectiveness. However, when he saw them for the first time, he was as shocked as his chief:

> Thus the first announcement of the enormous English Lines did not make a very great impression on us; however, everything was different from what we had expected in other places. The Lines were of such an extraordinary nature that I dare say there was no other position in the world that could be compared to them. In effect, it was not enough to encounter this formidable wall of rocks, supported on one side by the sea and on the other by an immense river. Behind it was a great capital with its arsenals, workshops, magazines to furnish all needs, workers of every description, artillery depots, and numerous batteries where large calibre guns were concentrated. Moreover, the population of the kingdom was

deluded and influenced enough to construct and defend all those fortifications; there was sufficient time to prepare them in advance, an open sea to feed everyone, and a large unencumbered fleet.

One might consider the question of just how the construction of the Lines by thousands of toiling Portuguese labourers could possibly have been hidden from the enemy. The truth is that it wasn't. The construction of the Lines might be called one of history's most open secrets. However, no-one quite appreciated just how the forts and redoubts actually linked up to form a continual defensive line from the Atlantic to the Tagus. Even Wellington's officers, including some engineer officers, never realised just what was going on until the Lines were actually complete. Whilst they could all see what was going on they never appreciated or imagined what the end result of all the work would be.

The story goes that one day Fletcher walked into a tent in camp and saw a plan of one of the forts lying on a desk. Without any fuss at all, he said simply, 'Ah! This is nicely drawn, but plans are very dangerous things,' and quickly tore it up. There was no sense leaving plans around for the enemy. It is almost as if a massive game of bluff was played out by Wellington and Fletcher: although they knew full well it would be impossible to conceal the construction work from the rest of the world, they hoped that nobody but themselves and Wellington's own very small 'inner circle' actually realised what the end result would be. In the event, nobody appears to have done so. As Jones, the historian of the sieges, wrote: 'Secrecy with respect to the extent and nature of works going forward was enjoined, and it is highly creditable to all concerned scarcely a vague paragraph respecting the lines found its way into public prints; and, notwithstanding the magnitude of the works, the invaders remained ignorant of the nature of the barrier raising against them, till they found the army arrayed on it to stop their further advance.'

The Signal Redoubt, situated on the Bayonet Ridge in the Pyrenees, another fine example of a Napoleonic earthwork. Nowhere along the Lines of Torres Vedras was there a position with this sort of altitude, although many of the forts in the Lines were of much greater strength than the Signal Redoubt itself.

Wellington's method of defence

In the words of the age-old adage, Spain is a country where 'large armies starve and small ones get swallowed up.' Never was there a finer example of this than when Masséna's invading French army arrived before the Lines of Torres Vedras. True, he was invading Portugal, but the two countries were, militarily, one and the same, and together they form the Iberian Peninsula. Although Napoleon may have referred to the Peninsular War as 'the war in Spain' or 'the Spanish ulcer', the two nations of the Iberian Peninsula proved as deadly as each other to the massive armies of Imperial France when they ventured south of the Pyrenees from 1807 onwards.

When Masséna invaded Portugal in the summer of 1810, Wellington had been planning for the eventuality for over a year: as noted, the Lines were begun in October 1809 as a result of observations made by Wellington during the same year and, indeed, in late 1808. But he knew full well that it would take more than just an extensive range of redoubts sited along an even more extensive range of lofty, impassable hills to bring the invasion to a halt. In order to thwart the French, Wellington knew he would have to call upon the people of Portugal to make a tremendous sacrifice, to give up and destroy their land, their farms, vineyards, mills, and their whole way of life in order to deny the enemy the very resources they required to sustain an invasion. Wellington's strategy was what we would call today a scorched earth policy, designed to starve the enemy rather than to defeat them in the field.

Wellington was only too aware himself of the adage about large armies starving in the Peninsula, and he resolved to see to it that Masséna's French army, if and when it ever did invade Portugal, would starve itself into submission in front of a defensive position. There was nowhere in Spain where such a position existed, and the war, once carried to the Lisbon Peninsula, would ultimately be decided by the abilities of the contending armies in the field. True, there were mountain ranges, but nowhere was there an area that afforded him the various elements that made the position north of Lisbon so immensely strong, where Wellington's own relatively small army could not be outflanked anywhere. The hills to the north of Lisbon were, therefore, a real gift, and there were few soldiers better qualified than Wellington, with his expert eye for the ground, to take advantage of their natural strengths and combine them with the sort of man-made defences that his head engineer, Fletcher, constructed throughout the 12 months from October 1809 to October 1810.

Under normal circumstances, strategy in siege warfare was dictated by the ability of the attacking force to sustain a siege and bring it to a successful conclusion, either by means of a storm, or by forcing the garrison to surrender, usually through starvation. It was also dictated by the prowess of the garrison to defend itself, and to buy enough time for itself to allow a friendly force to march to their relief. These were the kind of operations that Wellington undertook at Ciudad Rodrigo, Badajoz, Burgos and San Sebastian, with contrasting results. The French had likewise undertaken similar operations at Almeida, Zaragoza, Tarifa and, like Wellington, at Ciudad Rodrigo and Badajoz. When Masséna led his troops into Portugal in August 1810, we may well imagine Wellington planning for a similar scenario, with Masséna sitting down in front of the Allied position hoping to find his way through. Basically, the French invasion, post-Busaco (of which more later) developed into a siege operation, but with major differences.

When Wellington was considering his strategy for 1810 he fully appreciated that, at some stage, his army may well be called upon to make a retreat into

Portugal, and the last thing he wanted was for the retreat to degenerate into a repeat of Moore's retreat to Corunna in 1808–09. The construction of the Lines demonstrates Wellington's great ability to anticipate future events. At the heart of his strategy he would have to embrace the concept of siege warfare, with a prolonged stay behind his fortifications. But the unique situation of the Lines afforded Wellington the opportunity to engage in tactics, the sort of which could not effectively be used in conventional siege warfare, such as the aforementioned scorched earth policy.

Wellington anticipated making a stand somewhere along the route back to Lisbon. In the event, this stand was made atop the ridge at Busaco on 27 September 1810. Here, in what proved to be a very convincing victory for him, Wellington completely and bloodily repulsed a series of French assaults on his strong position to the extent that many historians have criticised him for not following up his victory and driving Masséna back towards Spain. But this was never Wellington's intention. His design was to draw the French deeper into Portugal where, if his overall scheme of things worked as well as he hoped – and his scorched earth policy was ruthlessly enforced – the French would quickly find themselves on the point of starvation. With the land stripped of its resources and with the onset of winter, they would soon be faced with little option but to retreat.

It was a well-thought-out strategy by Wellington, perhaps obvious today, but in the early 19th century it certainly had its critics, not least of whom were the members of the Portuguese Council. They considered the Allied retreat to be too hasty by far, verging on the cowardly – not that anyone actually came out and stated this – and claimed that it was a disaster to the country. There is little doubt that Wellington's policy was indeed a disaster for the country, but in April 1811, by which time Wellington had driven Masséna's starving, bedraggled army back over the Spanish border, he was able to tell the Portuguese people that he had delivered their country from the hated French invaders. Sadly, it is estimated that about two per cent of the Portuguese population, some 40–50,000 people, lost their lives during the period of Wellington's tenure behind the Lines, mainly through starvation and sickness.

This photograph illustrates perfectly the strength of the Lines. It was taken looking west from the area of forts 40–42 and shows the hills immediately to the south of the Alhandra to Bucellas road. Not content with the series of forts that dotted the skyline in this area, Fletcher saw to it that the hillside itself was scarped in order to increase the ascent towards the summit. It is still possible to see evidence of this today, visible immediately to the right of the two jagged points in the centre of this photo. By digging away at the slopes of the hill Fletcher not only increased the ascent but also denied the French any possible rallying point in the event of a failed assault. Note also the fact that this position formed part of the second line of defences.

THIS PAGE AND OPPOSITE **Two views** of the very deep ditch of Fort San Vicente. The fort itself is constructed on a commanding height, which could only be assaulted after a major effort. The ditch would have been a death trap to any French troops, had they managed to get into it. Indeed, it would have required scaling ladders and the sort of effort usually needed to assault regular fortresses in order to get into the place.

The scorched earth policy employed by Wellington involved the complete devastation of the countryside to the north of the Lines. After all, there was little point in his army occupying the Lines and still allow the French to help themselves to food and provisions from the land. Vineyards and crops were destroyed, mills dismantled, and the people ordered to destroy all stocks of food. Unfortunately, many of them understandably chose to ignore Wellington's order and hid their food instead. This was a foolish policy, for there were no troops more adept at discovering hidden food stocks than the French. Every bushel of wheat, every sack of flour or barrel of wine found by the French prolonged their existence in front of the Lines, thus causing Wellington real problems.

The vast majority of the population did, however, comply with his order and, after destroying all they could, hurried off to the south and to the relative safety of the Lines and Lisbon. Unfortunately, the conditions in the streets of the capital soon deteriorated owing to the massive increase in the population. It was here that so many of the people perished, for not even the Royal Navy was able to keep pace with the demands for food in the capital. Indeed, the majority of supplies brought in by ship went straight to the military.

No matter how effective the policy of scorched earth was, it would count for little if the French were able to attack the Lines successfully. Should they be able to do so the results for Wellington and his army would be nothing short of catastrophic. Barely 30 miles stood between the front line and the re-embarkation beaches on the Tagus, and so Wellington's arrangements for the actual defence of the Lines needed to be very effective indeed.

With the forts having been constructed and the natural defences augmented by his engineers, Wellington had to decide how to arrange both the garrisons and his main field army. One of the more unusual aspects of Wellington's strategy was to use his main field army, not as garrisons for the redoubts, but as a mobile force ready to move against any part of the Lines that may be breached by the French. The actual garrisoning of the redoubts was left to Portuguese troops, to the militia and the Ordenanza (an irregular armed force, akin to a national guard). The main Allied field army was then distributed with Hill's corps, consisting of two divisions, guarding the right of the Lines at Alhandra. Robert Craufurd's Light Division took up a position in and around Arruda, reaching out towards Alhandra in the east and Sobral in the west, whilst Picton's 3rd Division occupied Torres Vedras, watching the line of the River Zizandre. Leith's 5th Division was placed in reserve behind the heights south of Sobral, with Denis Pack's Independent Portuguese brigade occupying the great redoubt on the hill itself. The 1st, 4th and 6th Divisions, under Spencer, Cole and Campbell, occupied Zibriera, Ribaldiera, and Runa, their left flank resting upon Picton's right, and their right upon Leith's 5th Division. Three thousand cavalry were kept in reserve in the rear, whilst La Romana's 6,000 Spanish infantry were positioned between the first and second lines at Enxara doz Cavalleiros.

Arthur Wellesley, 1st Duke of Wellington (1769–1852). He commanded the Anglo–Portuguese army in the Peninsula in August 1808 and from April 1809 until the end of the war. Although he was criticised for his scorched earth policy prior to the occupation of the Lines, there is little doubt that this strategy proved immensely damaging to the French. He remains one of Britain's greatest soldiers.

OPPOSITE Two details from the plan of the Lines which appears in Jones' *Journal of the Sieges in Spain*. The section above shows the area from the extreme right-hand end of the first line at Alhandra, bordering on the River Tagus, to the second line as far west as the Montachique pass. The steep hills to the south of Bucellas can easily be seen, with forts 40, 41 and 42 at the eastern end of the range of heights. The section below shows the area of the Lines between Sobral and Torres Vedras.

While Wellington hoped never to have to defend the Lines, he had ensured that, should it be necessary, his men were more than ready to counter any French threat. The extent of the Torres Vedras position was little more than 30 miles wide, from the Tagus to the Atlantic, and with British infantry positioned along virtually its entire length, it should not, he reasoned, be particularly difficult to move his men east or west to parry any enemy attack, trusting in the ability of the redoubts to cause maximum damage to the French and to delay them long enough for the main field army to arrive. Given the excellent series of telegraph stations along the Lines, it would be relatively easy – provided the weather was good – to relay information along the Lines and through to Wellington's headquarters at Pero Negro in quick time. Wellington's army was certainly well versed in this sort of operation. Indeed, it should not be forgotten that, during the summer of 1810, the chain of outposts on the Côa and Agueda rivers was so effective that it took the Light Division just seven minutes to get under arms (15 in darkness) once an enemy attack had been detected – and this was along a 40-mile front. In fact Craufurd's system of outposts was so effective that the line, as Oman put it, 'quivered at the slightest touch.' Given the depth of supporting infantry within and behind the Lines, it was hoped, rightly so, that such an arrangement would be well within the abilities of Wellington's divisions.

In order to facilitate the movement of troops, several miles of lateral communication roads were cut into the reverse slopes of the hills, out of sight of the enemy. These roads, finally completed during 1811, formed a communication channel along the entire length of the position from the Tagus to the Atlantic, with direct communications from the rear line. Although the lateral communication roads were newly constructed, the roads between many of the redoubts remained as before, being old tracks, used by carts and other small-wheeled vehicles. Many were improved with paving stones, particularly those in wet areas, to prevent them becoming impassable. Fortunately, there were plenty of rocks and stones on the hillsides where the main communication roads were constructed, providing suitable material.

With artillery and garrisons in the forts, the rivers dammed, the valleys blocked, the approach roads broken up and destroyed, and with Wellington's main field army sitting secure and well-supplied behind them, the Lines presented an immensely strong and impregnable position. Notwithstanding this, Wellington was still concerned lest the French attempt to turn the right of the position by coming down the Tagus itself by boat. To counter any threat along the river, Royal Navy gunboats were anchored ready to receive the enemy.

All in all, the Lines of Torres Vedras were so immensely strong that there is little Masséna could have done to pass them. Wellington's precise arrangements combined with Fletcher's own meticulous supervision and attention to detail meant that it would take a superhuman effort at tremendous cost even to get close to a successful attack – although Masséna was tempted on more than one occasion to try it. Wellington (and Masséna) knew only too well that he needed to do nothing, other than ensure that he maintained constant vigilance. There was no need for any aggressive defence, the likes of which was required of a commander and his garrison during regular siege warfare when sorties were the norm. Wellington's greatest ally was starvation, and this could do more damage to the French than any sortie ever could.

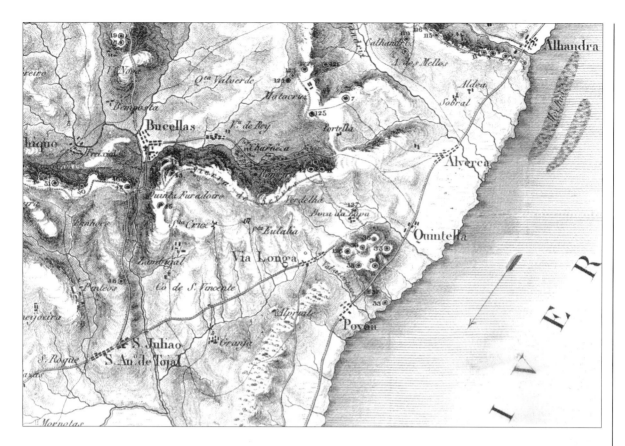

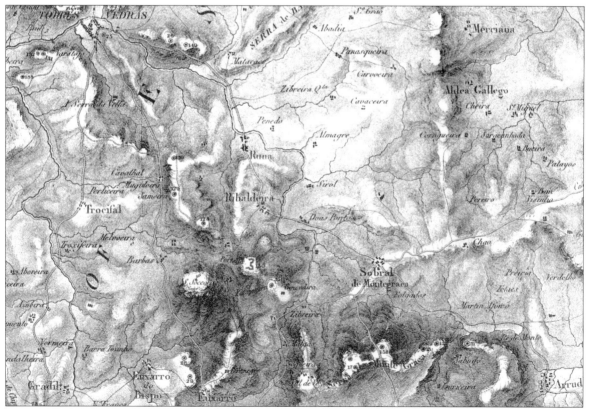

29

Looking west across forts 40–42, south of the Alhandra–Bucellas road

This illustration shows a large section of the Lines, and how strong the integrated defences were. Basically earthwork constructions, strengthened with stone, all three forts formed part of the second line of defences north of Lisbon. The forts are mutually supporting and completely cover the surrounding area.

Wellington's main field army is stationed in the rear, ready to move against any French attack.

Redoubts (simple earthworks) crown almost every hilltop in mutually supporting positions.

Communication roads have been cut into the hills to the rear, allowing quick access for Wellington's field army.

In addition to the guns in the forts, British artillery is positioned on the reverse slope out of enemy view. From here, they can fire upon both the enemy and the ground they may try to occupy.

The hillsides have been cut away to steepen the ascent to the crest for attacking troops. This also denies the enemy dead ground in which to reform in the event of a failed attack.

Signalling stations constructed at Alhandra, Sobral, Torres Vedras and Monte Soccora give early indications of enemy movements.

The direction of any possible French attack, uphill and under fire.

The open ground in front of the forts provides a perfect killing ground for the defenders whose fire, both from the slit trenches and from the main forts themselves, completely covers the enemy approaches.

Exterior slit trenches and flèches bring flanking fire on the attacking troops.

Fort 40 is an earthwork fort with strengthened stone ramparts; its angles allow flanking fire to be brought on all fronts. Most forts in the Lines were not star-shaped, but were of varying shapes and sizes: the elaborate designs were not deemed necessary.

FORT 42

FORT 41

FORT 40

WRY. 03

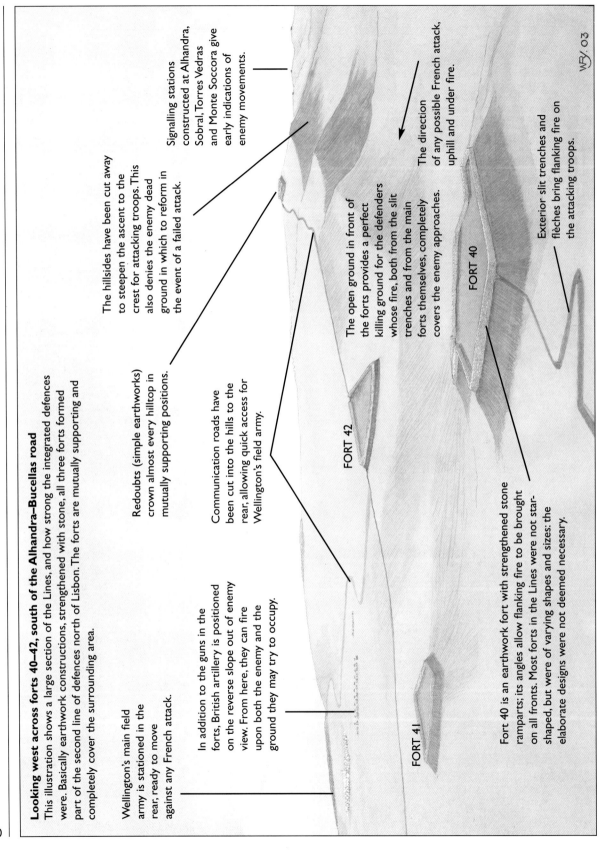

The forts

The elaborate star-shaped forts were a thing of the past when Fletcher turned his attention to the construction of the Lines. True, there was still scope for such forts, but it had long since been considered necessary to ensure that forts and redoubts were functional rather than simply pleasing to the eye. Generations of engineers had built their forts along the principles laid down by the great engineer, Vauban, whose star-forts adorned the length and breadth of France and the Low Countries. But the fixation with angles led many engineers to forget the basic principles of defence and thus it was that flaws began to emerge in the design and construction of many forts and even towns that had been encompassed within outwardly strong-looking but basically ordinary walls. As the engineer of the sieges, Jones, wrote: 'Many of the redoubts first thrown up, even some of the smallest, were shaped like stars, under the idea of procuring a flank defence for the ditches; but this construction was latterly rejected, it being found to cut up the interior space, and to be almost fallacious with respect to flank defence, the breadth of the exterior slopes being in some cases equal to the whole length of the flanks so obtained.' Indeed, the Great Redoubt at Sobral had no fewer than 23 'fronts', and by the time it was completed presented a very unusual shape indeed. The key factor was, however, that all approaches were covered, although Jones considered the redoubt to have been defective on account of a lack of flank defences.

One of the first considerations before building could begin was, of course, the ground. Not an obvious consideration, but it was if you owned the land

Fort San Vicente, Torres Vedras. A fine view of the ditch, glacis and the ramparts of the fort. Note the shape of the fort. It was constructed in such a way as to cover the approaches, and is a fine example of the way in which engineers turned away from the elaborate star-shaped forts of the previous century. The ditches and interior walls have been somewhat artificially preserved with concrete. It serves as a focal point for commemoration of the Lines of Torres Vedras.

used for the construction of a redoubt. Being situated so close to Lisbon meant that virtually all of the land was in use one way or another, whether it was used as a vineyard, olive grove or simply for grazing. Compensation was, therefore, a matter of serious concern for the local population and was indeed paid out to owners of olive trees and other trees felled in private woods. Compensation was also paid out to farmers whose crops were destroyed in the face of the French advance. Mill owners, whose mills had been dismantled or destroyed, were paid a monthly sum that equated to their average monthly income, in addition to which they were paid a sum for the restoration of their machinery afterwards. Unfortunately, the vast majority of individuals who lost property during the French invasion received nothing and had to bear the cost of the damage themselves

There were several other considerations to be made before construction could begin on the redoubts. First of all, Fletcher and his engineers, after carrying out a survey of the area, had to decide the purpose of the redoubt. In other words, was it there to prevent the enemy from taking up that same ground, or was it there in order to fire upon the enemy who might be attacking another point? The siting of the fort was made with careful consideration given to the direction of any possible enemy attack and on the accessibility of the surrounding area. In other words, it was no use building a fort on a height simply because the height happened to be there, particularly if the area around the height was open and easily accessible. If this was the case Fletcher had to ensure that the redoubt was supported by other works close by, works that, if possible, could be supported by natural obstacles. This was another consideration, for it was important that no work could ever be completely isolated by the enemy. The redoubt also needed to be large enough to support a garrison, and the size of the garrison, as we will see, was based upon the

These two bomb-proof traverses ran parallel to each other and allowed guns, men and ammunition to move freely along the fort at San Vicente with a relatively large degree of protection.

calculation of two men for each yard of frontage. The size of the fort dictated the size of the garrison therefore.

With the position of the redoubt having been decided upon, Fletcher's engineers had to trace out the shape of the fort. Having discovered that it was unnecessary to have elaborate shapes, Napoleonic engineers needed only to ensure that all approaches to the redoubt were covered and that the redoubt's security could not be compromised, at least not without a great deal of effort on the part of the enemy. And so, if a redoubt needed to be square, round, oblong, or even square with an oblong built on to it, then so be it. If angles were required it was a relatively simple business to work out the correct angle. Surveying equipment was easy to come by, but if not, an engineer only had to obtain a piece of rope and then divide it into twelve or nine equal lengths by way of tying a knot. Then, he would lay down the rope with four lengths along one edge, three along another and two along the final edge (five, four and three for a twelve-length rope). It was quite simple mathematics really. With the rope laid in this fashion, a right-angle triangle would be formed and thus the engineer would have his initial angle for the corner of his fort. This simple technique features in many manuals of the period. Experienced engineers would do this by sight. It may seem rather meticulous to have precise angles, but if a redoubt was incorrectly constructed it might have severe consequences for its occupants.

Many of the works were constructed on the summits of the many hills that comprised the Lines, giving the Lines a most formidable aspect. However, it was soon realised that this was, in fact, a flaw, for so steep was the ground in front of the works that it was extremely difficult, and in some cases nigh on impossible, for either artillery or musketry to fire downwards. However, their formidable situations gave the inexperienced and young Portuguese garrisons

This small chapel actually lies within the walls of Fort San Vicente, overlooking Torres Vedras. In the background can be seen one of the bomb-proof traverses.

Part of the ditch of the Great Redoubt, situated high on the hill to the south of Sobral.

A sketch of the interior of Fort San Vicente at Torres Vedras. The sketch, which appears in the correspondence of Lt. Rice Jones of the Royal Engineers, was obviously drawn some years after the Peninsular War. Nevertheless, it gives a good impression of the fort and the surrounding area. Compare the sketch with the photo on page 32.

inside them an immense amount of confidence that they might otherwise have lacked. The lofty situation of the forts also rendered them very secure from enemy musketry, it being impossible to get anywhere near to an elevation from which this would be possible. Nevertheless, it was still considered necessary to dig smaller redoubts or trenches in front of some of the larger, loftier forts, so as to protect the approaches from enemy fire or activity. The Great Redoubt at Sobral, for example, was protected on its flanks by smaller works.

The actual profile of each fort depended largely upon its situation, and the degree to which it was exposed to enemy artillery or attack. Generally, the only rule adopted was that the ditches should be at least 15ft wide at the top and 10ft in depth, whilst the top of the parapet should have at least 5ft command over the top of the counterscarp. Naturally, the thickness of the parapets did not compare with that of major fortresses. For example, nowhere, in any of the forts within the Lines, did the thickness of the ramparts exceed 10ft. Only

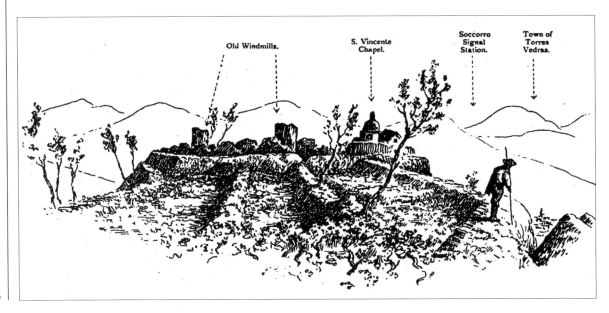

where there was a very real danger that a fort may be exposed to severe enemy artillery fire were the parapets strengthened. In fact, the parapets of many of the forts, particularly those situated on high knolls, well out of range of direct enemy artillery fire, were no more than 2ft thick, and were made of stone or piled-up spoil.

Another consideration – which was often neglected – was drainage. Forts number 101 and 102, situated at Oeiras, were so deep as a result of high parapets designed to protect the garrison, that, with no consideration having been given to drainage, they filled with water when, in September 1810, heavy rain fell. The subsequent work involved in first draining the forts and then cutting revetments to ensure they didn't flood again, took almost as long as the construction of the fort itself. Hence, drainage within the forts became a priority.

The construction of the forts involved three lines of workmen, one line of men digging out the ditch, and the other two piling up the spoil into ramparts and parapets. The earth was then hammered flat into a solid mass, (hopefully) strong enough to withstand enemy artillery. Some of the forts along the Lines were strengthened with stone, hauled to the hilltops by the peasantry. Today, it is still possible to see redoubts whose walls had been strengthened in this way, forts 40-42, for example. The interiors of the parapets were retained with sandbags or fascines. However, certain problems were experienced here. During the first winter the sandbags, which had become quite rotten, burst open, leaving the earth parapets to begin crumbling away. The fascines, on the other hand, were found to be a fire risk, or at least they were at first. Initially, they were formed of small branches and twigs which during the summer were like tinder. From then on, larger branches, without twigs or leaves, were used.

One of the primary functions of the redoubts of the Lines was, of course, to site and protect the guns that would fire upon any attacking enemy force. These were, naturally, constructed on the summits of hills in order that they could fire by line of sight. However, the purpose of some of the redoubts was to maintain guns which would fire, not on attacking troops but on any position they might try to occupy. In this case, a kind of 'reverse slope' principle was applied, whereby redoubts were constructed on the reverse slope of a hill, out of sight over the crest, with only the forward angle of the redoubt exposed to enemy view. It was important, of course, that these redoubts were sited in positions that could not be shelled from the rear. Otherwise, it was an effective

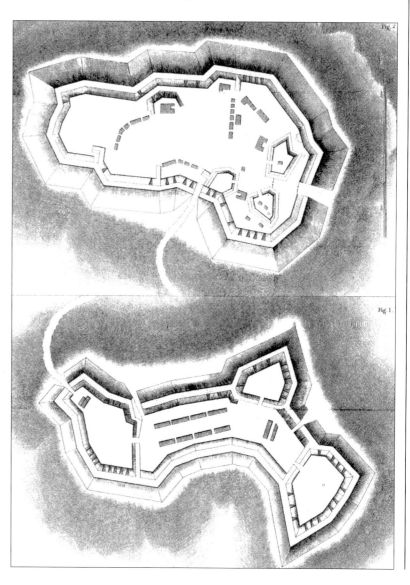

Two plans, taken from Jones' *Journal of the Sieges in Spain*, showing the Great Redoubt at Sobral (top), and Fort San Vicente at Torres Vedras (bottom). The elaborate star-shapes of the previous century have given way to a more practical, all-round defensive shape. Fort San Vicente actually consists of a group of forts, numbers 20 to 23.

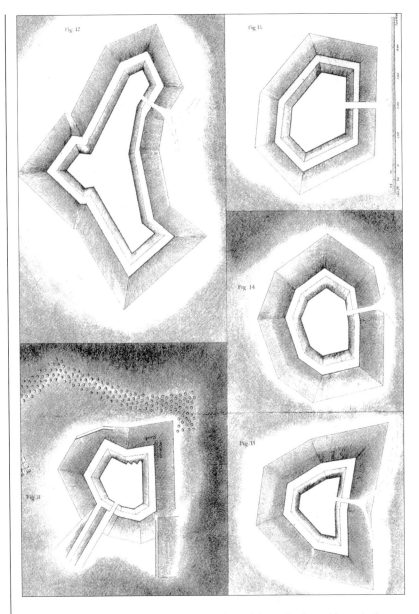

THIS PAGE AND OPPOSITE **More plans** from Jones' *Journal of the Sieges in Spain*, both showing the widely varying shapes of some of the redoubts within the Lines of Torres Vedras.

concept. As with Wellington's famous 'reverse slope' tactic of sheltering his infantry from enemy fire on reverse slopes, so these redoubts and their garrisons equally benefited from being positioned out of sight of the enemy artillery.

The guns themselves, along with ammunition and artillery stores, were provided by the Portuguese army from the arsenal in Lisbon, with Portuguese gunners manning them. It is a measure of the tremendous effort put in by the Portuguese workmen, that the guns were got into position after hauling them to the redoubts on the hilltops, having dragged them up truly rough tracks and roads. Jones, the historian of the sieges, wrote, 'It was gratifying to observe, on these occasions, by what persevering and patient labour the peasantry, with their rude means of transport (merely the common carts of the country pushed forward by oxen) succeeded in transporting 12-pounders into situations where wheels had never before rolled, and along the steep sides of mountains where horses would have been useless.' Some 3,208 Portuguese troops, regular and irregular, manned these guns, supervised by General Rosa, whose 'zeal and activity' smoothed all difficulties.

These were some of the main principles applied to the construction of the redoubts, although these were no different to those applied to the construction of redoubts and field works anywhere. It was really the positioning of the redoubts and the manner in which Fletcher utilised the natural strength and features of the area which made the Lines of Torres Vedras an impenetrable fortress.

Each of the forts required a garrison, of course, and the calculation of just how many men were required to man each redoubt was based upon having two men for each yard of frontage, not including the space needed for the artillery. By the time of the Lines' occupation some 29,751 men were required to garrison them, in addition to which there were 427 pieces of artillery. In 1812, by which time the Lines were considered to have been as perfect as they could, some 34,125 men were required to garrison the 152 redoubts, which in turn were armed with 534 guns.

A major consideration of any fort or redoubt was water. After all, no matter how strong a fort may have been, the garrison would not be expected to hold on for very long without water. In each of the redoubts within the Lines, casks of

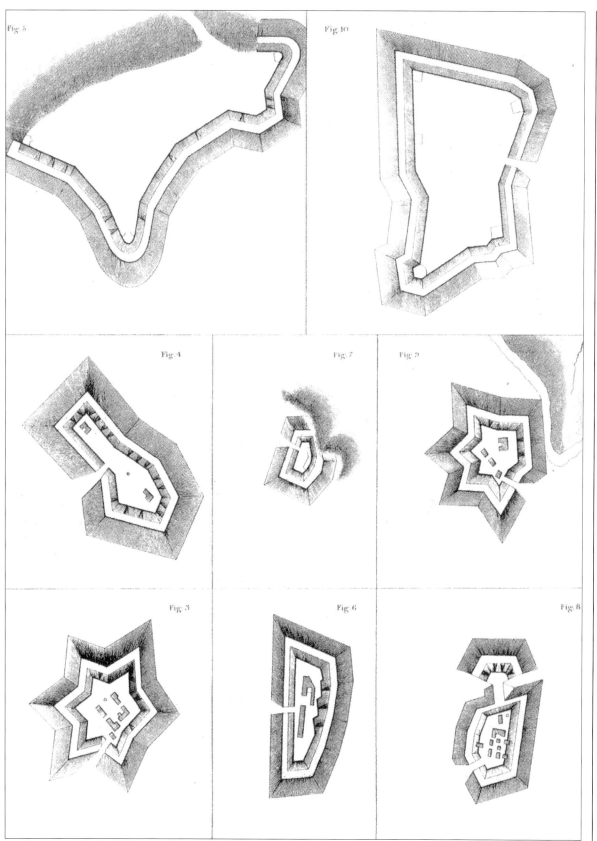

Fig. 5

Fig. 10

Fig. 4

Fig. 7

Fig. 9

Fig. 3

Fig. 6

Fig. 8

37

water were placed calculated to contain four quarts of fresh water per man for the garrison. In addition to water supplies, magazines were formed, made of splinter-proof timbers, 10in. by 8in. Drains were cut around them to keep the ammunition dry. Externally, the magazines were covered with 2ft of earth in sandbags, with tarpaulins spread over them to keep them dry.

Although the defence of the Lines was largely entrusted to the garrisons and artillery of the men manning the redoubts, it was also very reliant upon having Wellington's main field army in position in the rear, ready to advance and oppose any enemy threat. Communications were, therefore, of paramount importance and a series of telegraph stations were constructed which were worked by a party of seamen under Lieutenant Leith, of the Royal Navy. The telegraphs themselves consisted of a mast and yard, from which balls were suspended. Although the language of the telegraphs was that used in the Royal Navy, many sentences and phrases used by the army were introduced in time. The telegraphs were usually positioned seven or eight miles apart but because the mountainous nature of the area over which they were designed to work obscured their line of sight, five stations were needed and were built in order to communicate along the length of the first line at Alhandra, Sobral, Monte Soccora, Torres Vedras and in redoubt number 30 at Ponte de Rol. The lofty height of Monte Soccora, to the west of Sobral, dominated the area and proved to be Wellington's 'eagle's nest', from where it was possible, provided visibility was good, to see over vast distances. Indeed, it would have been impossible for the French to have advanced any formation of troops without being observed from here. Wellington himself rode forward each morning from his headquarters at Pero Negro, situated to the south of Sobral. Taking the newly-made road to the Great Redoubt (otherwise known as redoubt number 14), situated amidst the cluster of redoubts numbered 12 to 17 and 152, he would scan the surrounding area as far as the horizon, looking for signs of enemy activity.

It is interesting, looking back over the long period since the Lines were constructed, that, although we may consider them to have been impregnable, there were, nevertheless, British engineer officers who doubted whether they would hold the French back for one minute. Indeed, some thought it very likely that the Portuguese garrisons would run away at the first shot fired. Wellington himself, whilst appearing outwardly optimistic, was too professional a soldier not to have considered the prospect of French success. Wellington's army was, after all, the only field army Britain possessed and its preservation was an absolute priority. It would continue to be throughout the rest of the war. Therefore, he ensured that points of re-embarkation were fully surveyed and established. It was determined to make the primary point of re-embarkation close to Fort San Julian, to the west of Lisbon, where the guns of the fort could cover the beach. Here, a small bay, sheltered somewhat from the tides, afforded a reasonably safe place where boats could come and go, although even here the tides were notoriously bad, wave after wave crashing in against the beach. Nevertheless, between them Wellington and Fletcher decided that this small beach, covered by Fort San Julian, would be the point of re-embarkation should it be necessary to do so.

In addition to being called one of the best-kept secrets in military history, reference has also been made to the Lines being one of the cheapest. So, what was the actual cost in pure financial terms? According to Jones, the disbursements on account of the Lines, up until 6 July 1810, were around £60,000. By the time the Lines were occupied, the cost had risen to £100,000. By the end of the war, the cost of repair, preservation, and for communications, not to mention compensation claims, had pushed the cost up to around the £200,000 mark. The cost in human terms, lost lives, ruined livelihoods and such like, was immeasurable. But in purely military terms, this was a small price to pay for the total defeat of an invading French Imperial army.

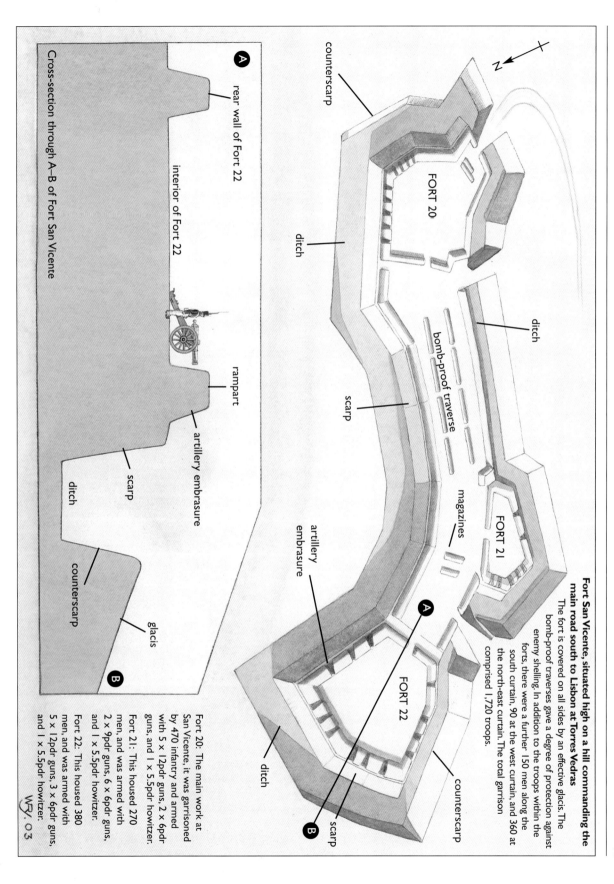

Fort San Vicente, situated high on a hill commanding the main road south to Lisbon at Torres Vedras

The fort is covered on all sides by an effective glacis. The bomb-proof traverses gave a degree of protection against enemy shelling. In addition to the troops within the forts, there were a further 150 men along the south curtain, 90 at the west curtain, and 360 at the north-east curtain. The total garrison comprised 1,720 troops.

Fort 20: The main work at San Vicente, it was garrisoned by 470 infantry and armed with 5 × 12pdr guns, 2 × 6pdr guns, and 1 × 5.5pdr howitzer.

Fort 21: This housed 270 men, and was armed with 2 × 9pdr guns, 6 × 6pdr guns, and 1 × 5.5pdr howitzer.

Fort 22: This housed 380 men, and was armed with 5 × 12pdr guns, 3 × 6pdr guns, and 1 × 5.5pdr howitzer.

Cross-section through A–B of Fort San Vicente

Life within the Lines

Life within the Lines of Torres Vedras was, quite simply, awful – at least for the unhappy Portuguese people who had been herded there having first been forced to destroy what amounted to their livelihoods. Theirs was the greatest sacrifice of all during the 1810–11 campaign, for they had little choice but to comply with Wellington's ruthless demands. Their olive groves, vineyards, and orchards were all destroyed in order to prevent the French from feeding themselves throughout what was expected to be a prolonged 'siege'.

As we have already noted, many peasants refused to co-operate and instead of destroying their crops they merely hid them, which was totally futile given the ability of the experienced French troops to sniff out food in the unlikeliest of places. The peasants' natural inclination to try and hide food annoyed Wellington immensely, but there was little he could do about it. In addition to this was the fact that some British officers failed to ensure that foodstocks were either destroyed or carried off. In his journal, John Burgoyne, a Royal Engineers officer, wrote:

> I myself was witness to messages coming to a general of a division, informing him of quantities of corn, &c., which they were forced to leave in such and such places, and which he would take no measures about, having no instructions on the subject. Such was the confusion and little warning the people had, that a cargo of English cheeses, &c., were left in Santarém or Villa Franca, quantities of turkeys and all kinds of poultry were left in the villages. So far from being in want, they [the French] must be living luxuriously … Even at Villa Franca, a town immediately on the Tagus, and only one league in front of our line, a very large quantity of grain was left. Therefore, all things considered, the idea of starving the enemy out of their ground is out of the question.

Burgoyne's view was certainly shared by others, but perhaps they failed to appreciate the size of the great French eating machine bearing down upon them, and the demands it would make upon the land, for it would not take long for starvation to set in, despite the amount of food discovered by Masséna's forage parties.

Wellington was not unaware of the sacrifices made by the people and knew full well what he was demanding of them. But Wellington was a professional soldier, and he cared little for popular opinion, of either himself or his policies, nor for the hardships experienced by the people. Wellington had to take a detached view of things, to examine the 'bigger picture'. It was his job to see to it that the French failed in their attempt to reach Lisbon, and that they were driven out unceremoniously as soon as possible. He didn't know how long it would take but that wasn't his problem. So long as the ships of the Royal Navy supplied his own men he knew he could remain to the north of Lisbon indefinitely. He simply had to see to it that his men were kept ever on the alert, that the defences were maintained in good condition throughout the winter, and that, in the event of a French attack, he had done everything possible to deal with it. Beyond that, he could do little more. If the people of Portugal thought that life was bad enough with their crops destroyed and with conditions in Lisbon becoming increasingly unpleasant, to say the least, then they should consider what it would be like if Wellington's strategy failed.

As Masséna's army marched deeper into Portugal the people fled in their thousands before it. Hundreds made off into the mountains, only to suffer a slow death from starvation. They risked this rather than return to their farms and suffer at the hands of the invaders. Thousands more made off along the roads to Lisbon. John Stepney Cowell, of the Coldstream Guards, witnessed their flight:

> It was a fearful sight to behold a whole nation's panic. It looked as though no soul that could move remained behind. The strong, the healthy, and the young were in arms; the old, the decrepit, delicate women and young children, were on foot in flight, wandering through forest, heath and mountain – in by-paths and cross-roads – over the face of their own fatherland, to avoid the destroyer. They carried on donkeys and mules, in their arms and on their heads, all of their small worldly chattels they could convey; the rest was buried or destroyed, and nothing was left to their foe but bare walls and empty habitations. The French might revel in a wilderness of dwellings – they were indeed masters of the soil, for none were left to share it with them.

Despite the hardships of life in Lisbon the people stuck with it, although at a terrible cost to themselves. Lisbon is not the largest of European capital cities today, never mind in 1810, and it is worth considering that no fewer than 300,000 people were herded into the area behind the Lines, the majority in Lisbon itself. Sanitation was at best poor, and coupled with the lack of food it is not difficult to understand why as many as 40,000 people perished in Lisbon during the winter of 1810/11.

Wellington also had to deal with the political fallout as a consequence of his retreat. There were many, particularly on the Portuguese Council, who considered the retreat to be unnecessary and at best too hasty. Why did Wellington not stand at Busaco, they asked? As we know, it was never his intention to do so, although this has been the subject of much heated debate ever since. We know that, in

A fine view of the ramparts of fort number 40, overlooking the road from Alhandra to Bucellas. The fort, basically an earthwork construction, was strengthened with stone, as were the other two forts close by, 41 and 42. All three forts formed part of the second line of defences north of Lisbon. The fort houses one of the few remaining magazines in the Lines. Deceptively strong, it completely covers the surrounding area.

Another view of fort number 40, clearly showing the way in which it covered the surrounding area. The steep approach would have made it difficult for the French to attack, whilst any attempt to outflank it would have been parried by the two forts nearby, 41 and 42.

August 1810, Wellington had already decided upon retreating to the safety of the Lines, stopping to fight a rearguard action along the way. We know this from one of his letters. But it must have been extremely tempting for him to launch his own attack at Busaco after the failure of Masséna's columns to assault his own position. It has been suggested that perhaps Wellington was bent on employing the Lines simply because he had to justify both the cost and his destructive scorched earth policy. After all, even considering the fact that the Lines were there to be employed throughout the remainder of the war if needed, Wellington might have found himself in a rather awkward position had he turned successfully and driven the French out after Busaco, leaving the Lines unoccupied and disused. But, as we know, the Lines were indeed occupied and used, and to great effect.

Once Wellington's men had occupied the Lines they quickly settled down to a prolonged period of inactivity. Initially, there was work to be done strengthening their respective positions. Although Wellington's main field army was not intended to remain a static force, it did, nevertheless, adopt a sort of siege mentality and so began improving their defences or seeing to it that any spot which may have been overlooked by Fletcher was made secure. For example, at Arruda, where Craufurd's Light Division was positioned, covering the Lines from Alhandra to Sobral, the men busied themselves in constructing a huge wall, some 40ft high and 16ft thick, which blocked the ravine to the west of the village.

Other than the work carried on to improve the existing defences, the daily lot of Wellington's officers and men soon developed into a regime of standing to in expectation of enemy attack, before standing down again to resume work

Wellington inspecting the French positions from the Great Redoubt at Sobral, 1811

Wellington would ride out every morning from his headquarters at Pero Negro so as to keep an eye on French movements. Here he is seen with members of his staff, including two Royal Engineers officers.

WRY. 02

on their positions. In his 'Memoranda Relative to the Lines of Torres Vedras', which forms part of his classic *Journal of the Sieges*, Major General John T Jones, himself a Royal Engineer who had worked on the Lines, described the daily routine of Wellington's army:

> Every morning, two hours before daybreak, the troops stood to their arms at the point of assembly of their several cantonments, as did also the garrisons of the works; Lord Wellington, in person, being in the fort on Monte Graca, in readiness to direct any general movement, according to the exigencies of the moment. The army thus remained under arms till a communication from every portion of the line, and ocular demonstration, had assured their commander that no change had taken place in the disposition of the hostile troops, nor any preparation been made for immediate attack; the several divisions and brigades were then ordered to resume their daily labours of strengthening their respective fronts, making lateral communications, improving the roads, sheltering and securing their outposts, &c. The weather was generally wet, and the duty irksome – still all supported it with cheerfulness, in the full confidence of annihilating their opponent, whenever the threatened attack should take place; but after a week had elapsed, expectation would no longer support itself, and the hope of an immediate and brilliant triumph subsided.

Whilst the men themselves may have been dismayed at the prospect of the campaign terminating without a decisive battle, Wellington could not have wished for anything better. His was an attritional campaign of almost Great War proportions, save for the fact that, unlike Earl Haig, Wellington had no need of costly forays against the enemy positions. No, all Wellington had to do was to sit tight, hope that Masséna was as clueless as he had hoped, and that logistics would begin to take their toll. In the event, this is exactly what happened.

Two more views of the forts covering the Bucellas road. The stone retaining wall has begun to crumble; not bad for a fort almost 200 years old.

The French made only a few half-hearted attempts to force the Lines, from 12–14 October, at Sobral. These were repulsed with relative ease, following which the men settled down into the monotony of their daily routine. However, it should not be imagined that the state of readiness amongst Wellington's men was anything less than extremely high. As Stepney Cowell wrote:

Another view of the hills to the south of the Alhandra–Bucellas road, giving a wider perspective of the defences of the second line. The photograph, taken from the area of forts 40-42, shows the scarped area in the centre, and the continuing series of hills further west, most of which were crowned with forts. It was an immensely strong position.

> We remained unmolested in our position, but in constant readiness to meet with prompt attention any visit our opponents may think proper to pay us; for this purpose our men slept in their accoutrements and we in our clothes. An hour before daylight each morning we stood to our arms; the baggage was packed and sent to the rear; clear roads, a clear field, and no 'impedimenta', was the order, and thus we remained till daylight made all objects distinct in the distance. Lord Wellington was generally with us almost daily before dawn, and generally took up his post with his telescope near our advance-piquets, or at the large fort which looked down on Sobral and the enemy's posts, till satisfied by personal observation in broad daylight, that no movement of attack ŵas contemplated by the enemy, after which he generally returned to Pero Negro.

For Wellington's men, life inside the Lines of Torres Vedras was, therefore, a mixture of tension, expectation of battle, disappointment, tedium and, at times, discomfort. Life for officers was no less uncomfortable, although those who managed to get off to Lisbon and stay in one of the many hotels – assuming they could find a room in the very overcrowded city – fared rather better. The hardest hit of all were, naturally, the Portuguese people. Short of food, living on the streets or in overcrowded accommodation, amidst disease and filth, theirs was not a happy lot. But they stuck it out and their sacrifices would eventually yield victory.

But what of the French? First of all, we should consider what Masséna intended to do once he discovered the Lines. His natural instinct under normal circumstances would have been to attack. But these were not normal circumstances. Never before had he encountered such a barrier as the Lines of Torres Vedras, and his well-documented reaction was one of complete shock. When one of his aides ventured the pathetic opinion that the Lines had been constructed in secret, Masséna snapped back words to the effect that Wellington did not create the mountains, asking why he had not been informed of their obvious natural strength. It appears that, for once, French intelligence had failed him, which is remarkable given the fact that the French had already occupied Lisbon once, when Junot marched into the capital in November 1807. It seems incredible that nobody left Masséna detailed reports of the topography north of the capital.

Masséna was not the first French officer to discover the Lines, however, that particular distinction falling to Montbrun, whose cavalry came up in front of Sobral on 11 October. During the next three days there was some sharp skirmishing in front of Sobral, the most severe coming on 14 October when Junot attacked Spencer's piquets to the south of the place. Little advantage was gained by the French, however, and when Masséna came up himself he at once realised just how difficult things would be over the next few weeks. As he rode forward with his staff, peering at the Lines through his telescope, a cannon sited in redoubt number 120 let loose a single shot at him which fell not too far away. Masséna took the hint and, after raising his hat to the men in the redoubt, took himself off to the rear, well out of range of the Allied guns. His very thorough reconnaissance quickly revealed the immense strength of the Lines and illustrated the folly of attempting a frontal attack on them. Indeed, one of his aides, Jean Jacques Pelet, was left to write in his journal, 'The enemy had worked on the Lines for more than a year and had gathered the peasants of the surrounding countryside there. They had conceived a perfect defence for

OPPOSITE Part of the old road constructed by the Portuguese to the Great Redoubt above Sobral. Wellington rode this way every morning to check on enemy movements. The road is in remarkably good condition, even after almost 200 years.

Wellington's headquarters at Pero Negro. During the period of the occupation of the Lines Wellington would ride from here every morning to the Great Redoubt at Sobral. A plaque commemorates Wellington's stay at the house.

British troops marching to take up their positions within the Lines. The natural strength of the hills can easily be discerned in this contemporary picture.

this country and had executed it completely to their advantage ... It was very difficult, if not impossible, to force the Lines without losing a dreadful number of soldiers.'

It was a real dilemma for Masséna. Having pursued Wellington to the very gates of Lisbon, his prize was about to elude him, and all because of a combination of natural and man-made defences. What was he to do? He was relatively isolated, with no real support, save for Soult in Andalucia and Estremadura, and despite having a strong army, numerically, he was at a loss as to how to attack the Lines without losing heavy casualties. There was nothing for it, he reasoned. He would wait for reinforcements to arrive before deciding his next course of action.

The problem was, of course, that this is exactly what Wellington had hoped for. He needed to do nothing other than to watch and wait for starvation to set in. It wasn't long before the first signs of this strategy began to bite. With the land stripped bare, and despite the French having found good supplies that had been hidden rather than destroyed by the Portuguese, starvation soon began to prey on Masséna's army, forcing the French to send foraging parties far and wide in search of food. Indeed, some of these parties were gone for as long as nine days whilst out foraging, and as the situation grew worse more and more men left their camps in search of provisions. The situation grew so bad, in fact, that one of General Clausel's staff was moved to report the following to Masséna:

General Clausel wishes to observe that during the daytime he cannot count on any other troops save those actually guarding the outpost line. The majority of the men are absent on raids to the rear, to seek for maize and cattle. The last detachment which came back to camp had been nine days away. Generals and soldiers agree in stating that for some time it has only been possible to collect a little corn with extreme difficulty. For eight days the troops have been living on polenta (boiled maize flour) alone, and of this they have received only half a ration. During the last four days the 1st Division has received only one ration of meat, which amounted to six ounces of goat's flesh.

Despite the immense problems in feeding themselves, the French hung on grimly, scouring the land for the merest of rations. Even Wellington was amazed at their ability to feed themselves. On 27 October, barely two weeks after Masséna had arrived at Sobral, he wrote: 'All the accounts which I receive of the distresses of the enemy for want of provisions would tend to a belief that their army cannot remain long in the position in which it is placed, and it is astonishing that they have been able to remain here so long as this.'

Despite the amazing ability of the French to exist in a land bare of resources, the situation was bound to tell on them eventually. So dire was their predicament that the problem of dealing with the Lines became of secondary importance. Whereas usually the French would have conducted themselves much in the same way that an army laying siege to a town would, their priorities soon became the feeding and subsistence of their army. Masséna and his staff may well have harboured hopes that an answer to the puzzle might be found but his men cared for little but their bellies. After four weeks, and with the situation growing worse by the day, Masséna decided to retreat north to Santarém where he hoped to be able to feed his army and await reinforcements. And so, on the night of 14 November 1810, his army began to drag itself away, undetected by the British piquets who, when dawn broke, could see nothing owing to a thick fog that had risen in the night. In fact, it was not until around 10am that the fog cleared and revealed to them that the French had moved off. Even then there was a delay in the British detecting the retreat, owing to the fact that the French had left behind them a line of stuffed dummies, which gave all the appearance of being real troops, until their stiffness caused the ever curious British to go and investigate. The news was immediately sent off to Wellington who quickly made his way to the great redoubt at Sobral. A swift examination of the French lines told him all he needed to know about the situation that presented itself before him. The French were on the run. The Lines had worked.

The British fleet prepares to re-embark the army, following the Battle of Corunna in January 1809. It was just such a scenario that Wellington hoped to avoid when he occupied the Lines. Nevertheless, he had earmarked a section of beach west of Lisbon, covered by Fort San Julian, where any possible re-embarkation would take place.

Aftermath

'If in the course of history of war a battle had taken place in which one side lost 30,000 men and the other a matter of hundreds, it would have echoed down the pages of history as the greatest victory ever won. But that, in fact, is the measure of the decisive nature of Masséna's defeat at the Lines of Torres Vedras.' This passage was written by the present Duke of Wellington, reflecting upon the achievements of his illustrious ancestor at the Lines of Torres Vedras.

It does indeed remain a fact that when Masséna crossed the Portuguese border shortly after the fall of Almeida in August 1810, he did so at the head of some 65,000 men. During his sojourn in front of the Lines he received a further 10,000 reinforcements. And yet, when he was driven unceremoniously back across the border into Spain in April 1811, his army numbered barely 45,000. So, what exactly had happened?

After the failure of Masséna to even try to break through the Lines, and with his army growing increasingly weak through sickness, he was forced to retreat north towards the River Mondego, where he hoped to maintain his position in Portugal until support arrived. If he hoped for support from Marshal Soult, at the time campaigning in Estremadura, he was to be sadly disappointed, for Soult's one and only intention was to lay siege to the great fortress city of Badajoz, which he took in March 1811. Masséna was totally isolated. In fact, the only reinforcements arriving in the Lisbon theatre were British.

On 5 March 1811, the very day that General Sir Thomas Graham was winning the battle of Barrosa, close to Cádiz, Wellington was about to achieve a greater and even more decisive victory north of Lisbon. With Masséna unable to sustain his army at Santarém and with no reinforcements forthcoming, the French commander began the long retreat north. Once the news of the French retreat reached Wellington, the Allied commander emerged to discover the French had finally admitted defeat and were making off in two columns; Marshal Ney, along with Junot and Montbrun's cavalry, was marching north towards Coimbra via Pombal, whilst a second column was making off towards Murcella by way of Thomar and Espinhal. Once the Allied commander was certain that Masséna was positively retreating with his entire army, he set off in pursuit. Unfortunately, Masséna had about four days' head start and made good time considering the appalling state of his army.

The route taken by the French as they retreated from Portugal was not difficult to follow: it was marked by burning villages, murdered peasants and atrocities the likes of which shocked even the British troops, whose own conduct, particularly after the storming of the major fortresses, has been condemned. The French themselves did not get off lightly. Indeed, hundreds of stragglers, wearied by the lack of food, were put to death, often a terrible one, by vengeful Portuguese guerrillas or by ordinary townsfolk, eager to settle the score with the hated invader. Every once and a while, British soldiers would come across French soldiers who had been tortured by Portuguese brigands, and were left to die. More often than not, these poor wretches begged their British adversaries to finish the job, but, of course, they were not able to. It was one of the most terrible episodes of the war.

The French army on the retreat. The reality of the situation when Masséna re-crossed the Spanish border was that he had lost almost 30,000 men, largely through sickness and starvation during the abortive invasion of Portugal.

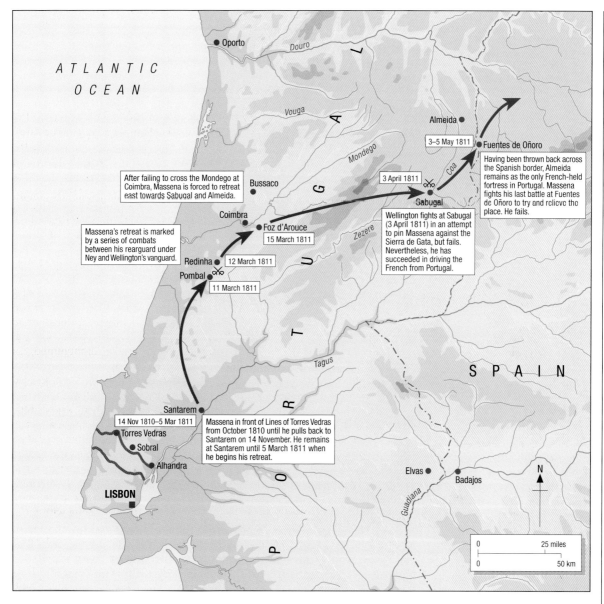

After failing to cross the Mondego at Coimbra, Massena is forced to retreat east towards Sabugal and Almeida.

Massena's retreat is marked by a series of combats between his rearguard under Ney and Wellington's vanguard.

15 March 1811

12 March 1811

11 March 1811

3 April 1811

3–5 May 1811

Having been thrown back across the Spanish border, Almeida remains as the only French-held fortress in Portugal. Massena fights his last battle at Fuentes de Oñoro to try and relieve the place. He fails.

Wellington fights at Sabugal (3 April 1811) in an attempt to pin Massena against the Sierra de Gata, but fails. Nevertheless, he has succeeded in driving the French from Portugal.

14 Nov 1810–5 Mar 1811

Massena in front of Lines of Torres Vedras from October 1810 until he pulls back to Santarem on 14 November. He remains at Santarem until 5 March 1811 when he begins his retreat.

Masséna's retreat, March–May 1811.

Wellington soon caught up with Ney's rearguard and on 11 March, there was a sharp fight in the town of Pombal, to which Ney set fire before continuing the retreat. The conduct of Ney's retreat drew much praise from several British commanders, including Sir Thomas Picton, who thought Ney handled the business well. When Wellington closed again at Redinha, Ney again turned, using Mermet and Marchand in another skilful rearguard action before falling back again. Condeixa was next, which was again severely damaged when Ney fired the place, thus causing further delays to Wellington. It was also the final chapter in the sad, sorry relationship between Ney and Masséna. Ill feeling between the two men had simmered away for the past few weeks during the campaign, and now, during the retreat, it boiled over when Masséna was almost captured by a patrol of the King's German Legion just outside Condeixa. Masséna, enjoying a spot of lunch with his staff beneath a tree, was stunned when the Allied cavalry suddenly arrived. Fortunately for him, the Germans were equally shocked to find themselves within a whisper of the commander-in-chief of the Army of Portugal. In fact, the cavalry were so startled they turned and made off, leaving a furiously

One of the two monuments to the fighting at Foz d'Arouce, one of the actions during Masséna's retreat from Portugal.

compromised Masséna to accuse Ney of deliberately trying to get him captured, after not advising him of his own movements.

There was yet another skirmish at Cazal Nova, but the most serious action came at Foz d'Arouce, on 15 March. Once again, the action involved the divisions of Mermet and Marchand, against the British 3rd and Light Divisions. In fact, the Light Division, still smarting after their chastisement at Ney's hands during their close escape across the Côa river on 24 July 1810, got full revenge for that near-calamitous day. The British vanguard arrived before Foz d'Arouce near dusk, and found the French preparing to camp for the night. Ney's arrangements for the security of his position were tardy to say the least and thus, when Wellington arrived on the scene to order an immediate attack, Ney was caught unprepared. The circumstances of his defeat at Foz d'Arouce bear uncanny similarities to that suffered by the Light Division on the Côa. His men were caught isolated on the wrong side of the river Ceira, with just a single partially destroyed bridge at their back when Wellington launched his attack. Whilst the Light Division attacked the French right, the 3rd Division came up on their left, threatening the escape route across the bridge. Panic set in, and then, suddenly, the French broke ranks and made off pell-mell towards the bridge, which collapsed beneath their weight. In the scrum to escape, many of the French 39th Ligne Regiment attempted to swim the river and were drowned. The regiment lost its prized Imperial Eagle, the golden bird that adorned their regimental flag. This was found some months later, washed up on the river bed.

After Foz d'Arouce, the French made for the bridge over the Mondego at Coimbra, but found it blocked by some Portuguese militia. Here, the Portuguese bluffed the French into thinking they were far more superior in number than they actually were after being summoned by the French to clear the way. The delay was long enough to allow British cavalry to come up and, fearing the rest of the Allied army might be close behind – they were not that far off, in fact – the French abandoned their plan to cross the Mondego and were forced to march along the south bank of the river instead.

A supply problem, owing to overstretched lines of communication, forced Wellington to halt for a while, which allowed Masséna to put some much-needed breathing space between himself and the snapping jaws of the Allied vanguard. However, Wellington was soon up with the French again, and on the foggy, rainy morning of 3 April clashed with them at Sabugal, in what was, for the numbers involved, one of the hottest contests of the war. Sent across the river Côa to try and get round the back of the French, a single brigade of the Light Division blundered into their flank instead, which brought an entire French division down on them. In what was a fine example of British staying power, Sidney Beckwith and his men more than held their own until the fog began to lift, exposing to full view their perilous situation. Fortunately, the lifting of the fog also revealed Wellington's army waiting and watching from the other bank, and the French were forced into making a hasty withdrawal.

Sabugal effectively marked the end of Wellington's pursuit of Masséna, and he was able to proclaim, with satisfaction, that the French invasion was over. 'The Portuguese nation,' he said, 'are informed that the cruel enemy who have invaded Portugal, and devastated their country, have been obliged to evacuate it, after suffering great losses, and have retired across the Agueda. The inhabitants of the country are therefore at liberty to return to their occupations.'

But although Wellington had driven the French from Portugal, there remained in the country one last enemy garrison which held on at Almeida, and it was the attempt to relieve the town that led to the Battle of Fuentes de Oñoro, on 3–5 May 1811. In the event, Masséna was unsuccessful in his attempt to break through to the beleaguered garrison and a few days later, Brennier, commanding them, and his men were forced to abandon the place and make good their escape through Allied lines. Masséna, on the other hand, could look forward to nothing more than a return to France, for he was relieved shortly afterwards by Napoleon and replaced by Marshal Auguste Marmont.

The Peninsular War would last for another three years, during which time Wellington and his men fought many great battles, the war finally coming to an end in April 1814 with Wellington emerging triumphant. However, it is important to stress that, whilst the Lines of Torres Vedras were never employed again by Wellington, they were never far from his mind, and he knew that, should they ever be required again, he could turn to them with confidence. Indeed, much of his strategy in the Peninsula subsequent to 1811 was based on this knowledge. For example, following the disastrous siege at Burgos, and the subsequent terrible retreat from there in October and November 1812, Wellington knew full well that, if the French pursued him beyond the Portuguese border, he could continue his retreat knowing that a great safety net was waiting to catch him. In the event, the French halted at Salamanca, and thus the use of the Lines was never required.

The Lines of Torres Vedras were, as we have seen, a total success. But in some ways they remain an enigma: we shall never know what might have happened if Masséna had attacked them. It is almost certain that whilst Wellington himself was relieved they did not, there were some Royal Engineers officers who must have been very curious to see the Lines put to the ultimate test.

The Battle of Fuentes de Oñoro, 3–5 May 1811. Ostensibly an attempt by Masséna to relieve the garrison of Almeida, it was the final battle of the French retreat from Portugal. It was also Masséna's last in Spain before he was recalled to France in defeat.

The Lines today

Considering the close proximity of the Lines of Torres Vedras to the Portuguese capital, Lisbon, the Lines remain in a rather good state of repair today. Indeed, it is possible to carry out a thorough examination of the Lines, from east to west, and still obtain a real feeling for their immense strength and their magnificent design. Like the series of French forts on the heights along the River Nivelle, the demands made on land have taken their toll on many of the forts, which have been destroyed or ploughed into the ground, but there remain a sufficient number of redoubts to make an exploration of the Lines a very rewarding experience. Each visitor to the Lines will, no doubt, find his or her own favourite redoubt or area. The redoubts at Sobral and Torres Vedras are naturally the most visited, but such is the extent of the Lines that visitors will find it more than rewarding to seek out the smaller works. Indeed, it is often these smaller, more remote redoubts that prove more satisfying.

The obvious place to begin any tour of the Lines is at Alhandra. Here, the visitor will find the huge memorial to Wellington's chief engineer, Sir Richard Fletcher, the man mainly responsible for the construction of the Lines. Due credit is also given however to Neves Costa, the Portuguese major often cited as being equally important in the concept of the Lines. The memorial takes the form of a huge column, topped with the figure of Hercules, and is built on the original site of redoubt number 2. From here a wonderful view to the east opens out over the Tagus, so that you can see how the gunboats of the Royal Navy would have prevented any attempt by the French to try and turn the Lines by way of the river.

Moving west, away from the Tagus and by the road to Bucellas, a visit to redoubts numbers 40, 41 and 42 is very worthwhile: here are examples of redoubts which have masonry ramparts, and one of the redoubts, number 41, even has a magazine. The redoubts are situated well off the main road and a considerable walk is involved in reaching them. However, it is certainly worth it. The three redoubts support each other perfectly and completely cover the surrounding area. Any advance by the French would have been seen almost immediately. The strength of the three redoubts is obvious to anyone today, but it is only when we consider that these three redoubts formed part of the second line of fortifications that we begin to appreciate the great depth of the Lines. After all, it would have taken a superhuman effort by the French to pass the first line of defences. To then have to deal with this second line only serves to remind us of just how formidable and all but impossible the task facing Masséna actually was.

The plaque adorning one side of the bottom of Sir Richard Fletcher's memorial at Alhandra. Unfortunately, his initial appears as a 'J'. A plaque on the other side of the memorial commemorates Neves Costa, the Portuguese officer who is often cited as being the person who devised the Lines.

Of course, the concept of the Lines of Torres Vedras was not based on man-made defences alone, and from these same three redoubts it is possible to obtain a wonderful view of how man helped nature to achieve his aims. By looking west along the forward crest of the ridge on which the redoubts are situated, you can see how the scarp of the crest was cut away by the Portuguese workmen in order to make the approach steeper than it already was.

As you journey west from Bucellas towards Sobral it is impossible not to notice just how many hilltops are studded with works, from small earthworks to larger redoubts. As you approach Sobral from Bucellas, you are greeted by a brown sign indicating the direction to Forte de Alqueidao. This, in fact, was the Great Redoubt, to which Wellington would make his way every morning from his headquarters at nearby Pero Negro. If ever we needed reminding of the massive job carried out by the Portuguese workmen, it is here, for the road they built to the redoubt still survives today. The ground was cut and thousands of stones laid to facilitate the movement of men, horses and artillery. It takes a good 15 minutes or so to reach the redoubt, which today lies amidst thick woods, but the view is tremendous. Although bushes and trees have tended to obscure the works themselves, it is still possible to find the original traces of the works, the ditches and the forward flèches that were dug to cover the approaches to the redoubt. Today's Portuguese army have constructed a fine viewing platform in the centre of the fort, with tiles placed all round the inside indicating the positions of the various forts in the area. It is a first-class viewing point. Sobral looms in the distance at the foot of the position, and it is easy to see why, with the French in possession of the town, Wellington considered the redoubt so important. Two other forts are situated nearby, although these are thickly covered by bushes and trees too.

The memorial to Sir Richard Fletcher at Alhandra. Situated in what was once Redoubt Number 2, the memorial affords a fine view out over the River Tagus, and north towards Santarém.

A visit to Pero Negro itself is a must. It is possible to travel the Iberian Peninsula and visit scores of buildings used by Wellington. Fuenteguinaldo, the convent of São Jão, St Jean de Luz, and Freneida are just a few. His headquarters at Pero Negro are very easy to find. Situated on a hill to the east of the town, an imposing yellow house, surrounded by a high wall, is distinguished by a plaque which informs visitors of Wellington's (or Wellesley, as the plaque states) stay there during the occupation of the Lines. An atmospheric place, it is easy to imagine the comings and goings of Wellington and his staff throughout the late autumn and early winter of 1810. Leaving Pero Negro to the east, and crossing the railway, a short drive of about one mile south brings you to a small clutch of houses, situated on the left of the road. The first house, Casal Cachim, once a fine-looking building but now rather dilapidated, served as the headquarters of Marshal Beresford.

A short distance along the road south from Pero Negro lies the Casal Cachim. This was Beresford's headquarters during the winter of 1810/11. The house is somewhat dilapidated today, although a plaque happily recalls Beresford's occupation of the premises.

Although not mounting any redoubt, Mount Soccora is well worth a visit too. Situated about two and a half miles to the north-west of Pero Negro, it provided Wellington with a magnificent observation point, upon which a telegraph station was placed. A very poor unmade road winds its way to the top and although it is possible to drive a car to the top (I've done it a few times – although I made sure it was a hire car, and not my own!) visitors should think twice about doing it. The road is steep in places and can be very tricky if you're not used to off-road driving.

Naturally, no visit to the Lines would be complete without visiting Torres Vedras itself. There is a small but good museum in the town which houses many artefacts dating from the Peninsular War, some good dioramas and, of course, much on the Lines themselves. A large obelisk stands in the centre of the town, commemorating the victories of the Anglo-Portuguese Army at Rolica, Vimeiro and Busaco. The principle reason for visiting the town, however, is to explore Fort San Vicente, the strongest and best-preserved fort in the Lines. Today, it provides the focal point of commemoration, and plaques mark the visit by the present-day Duke of Wellington. Fort San Vicente stands on a hill, high above the town, and encompasses an old chapel within its ramparts. It actually consists of three forts joined together. Numbered 20, 21 and 22, they have long since been restored and somewhat artificially strengthened with stone and concrete, but their extremely deep ditches and bomb-proof traverses provide ample evidence of the fort's immense strength. Indeed, the fort was designed to hold some 5,000 men and mounted no fewer than 40 guns. It was also protected by fort number 27, which was in effect a Moorish castle, built to command the road from the north. Like Wellington, the Moors also appreciated the strategic importance of Torres Vedras and built their own castle to protect the road.

There are scores of redoubts dotting the hills today, and visitors will, no doubt, discover their own favourites in time. The ones referred to above are only a few of the main ones. Driving around the area you will never cease to be amazed by the strength of the Lines. But it should not be forgotten that Wellington was taking no chances, and in the event of a French breakthrough had ordered Fletcher to come up with a suitable place where the British army might re-embark in safety. The place decided upon was on a small beach immediately to the east of the very powerful Fort San Julian, which itself is situated to the west of Lisbon on the road to Cascais. Fort San Julian is still a military establishment today and is also a government hospitality centre. A strong fort was built on a hill just to the north of the fort in order to cover the re-embarkation of the troops, but it was the guns of Fort San Julian that would have provided the most effective cover. Looking at the waves crashing in on the shore of the Tagus it is worth contemplating the difficulties the British troops would have faced in getting into the small boats: they would have been tossed about, as they had been when the army came ashore at the River Maceira prior to the battle of Vimeiro. In order to facilitate the re-embarkation, four jetties were built, much to the amusement of the locals who thought they would be swept away in no time. However, the jetties survived for some years after the war had ended.

Wellington ensured that the arrangements made at Fort San Julian, and on the third set of Lines which covered the re-embarkation area, were carried out as thoroughly as at any point in the Lines. Nevertheless, it is worth taking a

The front entrance to Beresford's headquarters, the scene of great coming and going during the winter of 1810/11.

moment to try to imagine the scenes on these beaches had Wellington been forced to pull back from the Lines and re-embark his men in the ships of the Royal Navy.

It is also worthwhile visiting Santarém, a pretty town in its own right, but from November 1810 until March 1811 Masséna's headquarters. It was here that the French commander sat and pondered over the various courses of action open to him, none of which yielded anything other than frustration and misery for both himself and his army. The area round Santarém was stripped bare of resources, and when Masséna himself withdrew north, he left behind a town which had been completely sacked by its former inhabitants.

There is also a fine military museum in Lisbon itself, with rooms dedicated to the Peninsular War and the Lines. The museum, once the royal arsenal, also houses one of the finest collections of arms, armour and equipment in Europe. The museum has a direct link with the Peninsular War and in particular the Lines of Torres Vedras, for it was from here that the majority of the guns that were placed in the redoubts along the Lines were brought. The building is situated on the riverfront: allow a few hours if you intend visiting it. Finally, it should be mentioned that many of the redoubts that still exist today are situated on private property and as such visitors should take care not to trespass or to cause any damage.

Definition of key terms

The following definitions of fortification terms come from *Instructions for Officers of Infantry, showing How to Trace and Construct all sorts of Field Works; As also the best method to put Churchyards, Churches, Castles, Villages, Towns, &c. in a State of Defence*. The book was written by General F Gaudi, and translated into English by C Marorti de Martemont. Published in 1804, the book describes in great detail everything an engineer officer needed to know about the principles of defence. It is only one of several such manuals published during the early 19th century, but was extremely popular with British officers: the extensive list of subscribers makes interesting reading in itself. The following list of terms forms part of the manual. Some of the more peculiar terms have been edited out, others simplified, but on the whole these definitions appear exactly as they were published.

Fortification

Fortification is the art of putting any place or post whatever in a favourable state of defence; it implies also the method of attacking and defending the same.

Permanent fortification is particularly applied to the erecting, attacking, and defending of such places as are properly denominated fortresses, and which are constructed in time of peace, to the purpose of protecting a whole country against future attack or irruption of the enemy.

Temporary fortification, which is called **field fortification**, has a similar object to that of permanent fortification, namely to procure the means of enabling a small number of men to defend themselves with less danger against a greater number, who attack them; but it differs in this one point, namely, that field works are only intended to exist for a short limited period, that they are frequently constructed in the greatest hurry, when many requisites are wanting, and sometimes in the presence of the enemy.

Various kinds of field works

A **fort**, generally so called, is a place surrounded by a parapet. Forts, however, receive different appellations, according to their figure, and to the number of their sides or faces.

A fort, whose figure is a circle, is called **a round or circular fort**.

A fort is said to be a triangular, square, pentagonal or hexagonal fort, &c. according as it has three, four, five or six, &c. sides or faces.

When the circumference of a fort is composed of lines forming alternate salient and re-entering angles, it is called a **star fort**, and likewise receives the appellation of a square star fort, of a pentagonal or hexagonal star fort, &c. according as its salient angles are four, five, six, &c. in number.

All field works that have no flank defence of their own are called **redoubts**.

Half-redoubt, *flèche* or **arrow**, is a small work with only two faces, which form a salient angle.

Redoubts *en crémaillère* are so denominated from their figure, which resembles a pot-hanger, or the tooth of a saw.

Têtes-de-pont are works that are made of various forms, and intended both to cover bridges of communication, and to contain the troops which are destined to protect the manoeuvres of a body, either when forcing their passage over a river, or when re-passing it on their retreat.

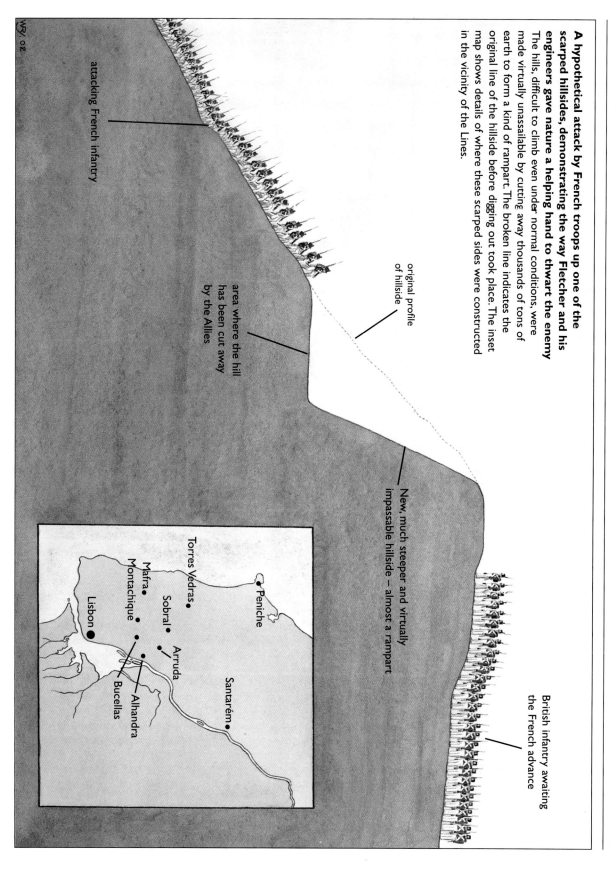

A hypothetical attack by French troops up one of the scarped hillsides, demonstrating the way Fletcher and his engineers gave nature a helping hand to thwart the enemy The hills, difficult to climb even under normal conditions, were made virtually unassailable by cutting away thousands of tons of earth to form a kind of rampart. The broken line indicates the original line of the hillside before digging out took place. The inset map shows details of where these scarped sides were constructed in the vicinity of the Lines.

attacking French infantry

original profile of hillside

area where the hill has been cut away by the Allies

New, much steeper and virtually impassable hillside – almost a rampart

British infantry awaiting the French advance

Torres Vedras

Peniche

Mafra

Montachique

Sobral

Lisbon

Arruda

Santarém

Bucellas

Alhandra

WR/ 02

Obstacles

A **parapet** is an elevation of earth thrown up around a fortified place, and which, owing to its height and thickness, serves to protect the men who are to defend it against every attack from the enemy, and especially against the fire of his musketry and artillery. Now, the parapet being made of loose earth, it could not possible stand long, if its outer and inner sides were carried up perpendicular to the horizon; therefore, it is proper they should make an acute angle with the horizontal base of the work. The slope of the sides is called the interior and exterior slope or talus of the parapet.

The upper surface of the parapet is called the **summit** or **crown**; it must be made sloping towards the country, otherwise the enemy could not be hit from behind the parapet, when advanced within a moderate distance from the work. The slope of the upper surface is called the **slope** or **talus** of the summit of the parapet, or simply, the slope or talus of the parapet.

As the height of the parapet exceeds that of the men who are to defend the work, an elevation of earth is made immediately behind, and at the foot of it, which is called the *banquette*; this elevation, which the soldiers mount when they are to fire, enables them to fire over the parapet. To render the ascent of the *banquette* more easy, you must give a slope to its inner side, which is called the slope or talus of the *banquette*.

A small space must be left between the foot of the parapet and the ditch, which is called the **berm**, and intended to prevent the giving way of the scarp, which would have too great a pressure to sustain from the parapet, if the exterior slope of this latter, and the scarp formed but one continued surface.

It is customary to make a **ditch** on the outside of the parapet, in order to procure the earth that is required for the formation of the parapet, as also to oppose an additional obstacle to the enemy.

Both sides of the ditch must have a slope or talus; that of the inner side is called the **scarp**, and that of the outer side, the **counterscarp**. The **covered way** is a space left between the counterscarp and the glacis.

The **glacis** is a kind of parapet raised up beyond the ditch, the summit of which ought to be continued outwards in a gentle slope, and gradually decreasing till it meets the surface of the ground.

We call an advanced ditch a **second ditch**, formed in front of the former beyond the glacis.

A covered way practised beyond an advanced ditch is called an **advanced covered way**.

Additional obstacles

Besides the parapet, the ditch, &c. other obstacles may be presented to the enemy to check his progress, or impede him in his attempt to become master of a work. These are as follows:

Palisades, a name given to one or several lines of square stakes, pointed at the top, and driven two or three feet deep in the ground. These are joined together near the top with laths, which are fastened to them with rivetted nails.

Fraises are a kind of palisades, placed nearly in a horizontal direction (by which is meant, that the pointed ends are rather inclined towards the bottom of the ditch) in the revetment of the parapet.

Chevaux-de-frise are square beams through which stakes four inches thick are driven in an oblique direction, so as to cross each other, and to stretch out as much on one side as on the other, in such a manner that two rows of those stakes touch the ground, and the other two are upwards.

Trous-de-loup are holes pointed at bottom, in the middle of which a stake pointed at the top is two feet lower than the top of the hole; *trous-de-loup* are placed in front of the parapet, and about sixteen or twenty feet from the counterscarp.

Crows feet, or *chausse-trappes* are pieces of iron with four points, each a few inches, and so formed that in what manner soever they may be thrown, one of the points always remains upwards.

An **abattis** is formed by means of trees cut down, placed close by and over one another, so that their heads are presented towards the enemy and their trunks towards the work.

Fourgasses are small mines whose chamber is sunk but a few feet deep.

Various definitions

Pieces of cannon placed adjacent to one another behind a parapet form a **battery**. There are two different sorts of batteries, namely, batteries with embrasures, and batteries *en barbette*.

Embrasures are openings so practised in the parapet that the guns may fire through them. Where cannons are to fire over a parapet without embrasures, we call it **firing *en barbette***.

Enfilade. A work is said to be enfiladed when a gun may fire into it, so that the shot may run all along the inside of the parapet.

By **cross fire** is meant the fire of two or more adjoining sides crossing each other.

A **breach** is an opening made in a wall or parapet with cannon or mines, sufficiently wide for a body of troops to enter into the work and drive the enemy from it.

Command. When a hill or rising ground overtops any work of a fortification, and is within cannon shot, that hill or rising ground is said to command that work.

A **revetment** is a lining generally made in the field, and composed of fascines or sods, sometimes of hurdles of willow trees woven together in the manner of basket-work, the object of which is to support the interior, and sometimes the exterior side of the parapet.

A **traverse** is a parapet made within field works to cover the entrance, or when there are any hills or rising ground from which the inside of the works may be discovered.

A **fascine** (common) is a kind of bundle made of branches tied in two or more places, of about six or eight inches diameter.

A *saucisson* is a fascine which is longer than the common one, and which has in general one foot diameter. *Saucissons* are used for the revetment of batteries, parapets, and for repairing breaches, &c.

A **gabion** is a kind of cylindrical basket open at both ends, of about three feet wide, and from three to six feet high, which is filled with earth.

Loop holes are square or oblong holes made in a wall to fire through with muskets.

Communication is a passage from one work to another, and generally covered by a parapet or palisades on each side.

A **Place of Arms**. A proper place for collecting the men and materials, as also the engines of every description destined for the attack or defence of a post.

A **block house** is a building of timber erected in the middle of a work to shelter the garrison, and especially the guard, from bad weather; it ought to be roofed with beams, over which earth and sods are heaped a few feet thick.

Further reading

There have been surprisingly few books written about the Lines of Torres Vedras since the Peninsular War ended in 1814. In fact, there are really only two works on the subject, and one of those was written as late as 2000. It was not until 1846 that the first great work on the Lines of Torres Vedras was published. Major General Sir John T Jones's *Journal of the Sieges Carried on by the Army under The Duke of Wellington in Spain, during the years 1811 to 1814*, was first published in 1814 in a single volume, but in 1846 a three-volume edition appeared, massively enlarged and with the addition of a whole volume focussing on the Lines. Jones had been a Royal Engineer officer in the Peninsula and was thus more than qualified to give an account of the proceedings relative to the Lines and, indeed, to the other sieges in general. Jones gives a complete and extremely thorough appraisal of the Lines, from the country to the north of Lisbon, the planning, the construction, the cost and the effects on the population. He is critical where necessary and gives a completely professional view of the Lines.

Perhaps reflecting just how much historians have underestimated their importance, it was not until 2000 that the next major volume on the Lines appeared. Written by John Grehan, and simply entitled *The Lines of Torres Vedras: The Cornerstone of Wellington's Strategy in the Peninsular War 1809-1812*, the book differs from Jones' work in as much as it addresses the wider issues involving the construction of the Lines. For example, the book goes into the original conception of the Lines and it outlines in some detail how Wellington's campaign in 1810 was heavily reliant on their construction and, more important, their completion. The book also tackles the sensitive issue of the sacrifices made by the Portuguese people and the cost in terms of destroyed livelihoods and the thousands of deaths through disease and starvation. We also see how Wellington could, perhaps, have avoided using the Lines at all, particularly after Busaco. The author also argues the case that Wellington's strategy throughout the years subsequent to 1810 was planned with the knowledge that the Lines would always be there should it ever be necessary for him to retreat.

In 1986, the British Historical Society of Portugal published its own guide to the Lines. Written by A H Norris and R W Bremner, *The Lines of Torres Vedras* is an extremely useful, if brief, guide to the Lines both from a visitor's viewpoint and an historical one. The authors had the advantage of much local information, of course, but put it to great use in what is a very helpful book, giving a complete guide to the redoubts' locations and their state in 1986.

There are several collections of papers in the archives of the Royal Engineers Museum in Brompton, Chatham, Kent, and in the RE's library itself. Otherwise, there are few other books directly concerned with the Lines, the two books named above being the major works. Of course, there are scores of journals and letters that refer to the construction of the Lines, their occupation and the French retreat. A first-rate bibliography can be found in John Grehan's *The Lines of Torres Vedras*. One diary of note is Rice Jones' *An Engineer Officer under Wellington in the Peninsula*, edited by H V Shorne. Published by Ken Trotman in 1986, Jones' book is full of very interesting sketches of some of the redoubts including the Great Redoubt at Sobral and Fort San Vicente. It is interesting that whilst Jones could not fail to notice the extensive works being carried out across the Lisbon Peninsula, even he had no idea just how they would eventually link up, emphasising the secrecy surrounding their construction.

The French view is perhaps best represented in Jean Jacque Pelet's book, *The French Campaign in Portugal, 1811*. Although edited by the very pro-French Donald Horward, Pelet's own account gives us a marvellous insight into French thinking, their shock at seeing the Lines for the first time, and the growing desperation within their camps as they sat there, unable to find a solution to the problem of breaking the Lines.

Another very important work is, of course, Wellington's *Despatches* and *Supplementary Despatches*, which were published in 1832 and 1857 respectively. In these multi-volume works are to be found the majority of Wellington's own correspondence relating to all matters concerning the Lines and their construction. His *General Orders*, published in 1839, are useful also.

Good accounts of the Lines, their construction, but mainly their effects on the Peninsular War can be found in the three classic accounts of the war: William Napier's six-volume *History of the War in the Peninsula*, published from 1828 onwards; Sir Charles Oman's seven-volume *History of the Peninsular War*, published from 1902 onwards, and in volumes 6–10 of Sir John Fortescue's *History of the British Army*, published between 1910 and 1920.

Index

Figures in bold refer to illustrations